I0111237

The
Holy
Scriptures

THE WESLEYAN THEOLOGY SERIES

The
Holy
Scriptures

Stephen G.
Green

f▸

THE FOUNDRY
PUBLISHING°

Copyright © 2021 by Stephen G. Green
The Foundry Publishing®
PO Box 419527
Kansas City, MO 64141
thefoundrypublishing.com

ISBN 978-0-8341-3983-1

All rights reserved. No part of this publication may be reproduced, stored in a retrieval system, or transmitted in any form or by any means—for example, electronic, photocopy, recording—without the prior written permission of the publisher. The only exception is brief quotations in printed reviews.

Cover design: Arthur Cherry
Interior design: Sharon Page

Unless otherwise indicated, all Scripture quotations are from the New Revised Standard Version Bible (NRSV), copyright © 1989 National Council of the Churches of Christ in the United States of America. Used by permission. All rights reserved worldwide.

The following copyrighted version of Scripture is used by permission:

The Holy Bible, New International Version® (NIV®). Copyright © 1973, 1978, 1984, 2011 by Biblica, Inc.™ Used by permission of Zondervan. All rights reserved worldwide. www.zondervan.com. The "NIV" and "New International Version" are trademarks registered in the United States Patent and Trademark Office by Biblica, Inc.™

Library of Congress Cataloging-in-Publication Data
A complete catalog record for this book is available from the Library of Congress.

The internet addresses, email addresses, and phone numbers in this book are accurate at the time of publication. They are provided as a resource. The Foundry Publishing® does not endorse them or vouch for their content or permanence.

To my children: Stephanie and Michael
I love you both!

Contents

Acknowledgments

It takes more than a single lifetime to read the Bible well. Therefore, we must read these sacred stories and poems with others. I began the journey of reading the sacred texts before I was able to actually read. My parents placed at the center of our lives the family Bible. My father, who was also my pastor, would read long passages of Scripture to us every night, and then we would all add our words of interpretation, confession, and prayer to these sacred words of witness. These practices narrated my brothers and me into the strange world of God's story. That story-formed world was not simply long, long ago and far, far away, but it was our world. It was a world we would wake up to every morning and move about during the day. It was a good world of creativity, love, faithfulness, mercy, and redemption. I really did not choose this world, but this world seems to have chosen me. Don't get me wrong—I attempted to flee this world, but I was as successful as a fish fleeing the water. It was in the air I breathed and in paths I traveled.

These paths carried me on a quest to read these ancient words with clarity and integrity. This pathway guided me to graduate school, where I learned ancient languages, philosophical methods, Christian heritage, theological arguments, and the critical methods of biblical exegesis. A quandary developed: What is one to do when one's world is confronted by the historical-critical method? Clearly, resistance is one option. But a person can never unlearn what was learned. Must a person then give up the old story? That is like asking the question, Can a human being develop gills and breathe in the water? Or can a person sprout wings and fly like a bird? This predicament is actually asking, How is one to believe in the inspiration of Scripture and still understand the Scriptures historically? The chapters in this book form an argument attempting to answer this question.

As you can see, I've read texts in a variety of communities: the church, the academy, and with the great cloud of witnesses who have lived in both of these communities of memory. I have many to thank for this journey. Most notably are the teachers who have patiently walked with me in times of confusion and uncertainty. Many of these mentors I have mentioned by name in my commentary on Deuteronomy. But there are two groups I want to acknowledge in this opening statement: the many authors I have read and the many students I have taught. The bibliography at the end of this book is but a small sampling of those who have shaped my journey of reading the Bible Christianly. I do not use many quotations in this book, other than those from the Scriptures. Yet the ideas and concepts of great thinkers have crept into my consciousness. Some of these thinkers I would call exemplars of all I hold dear and attempt to do as a faithful reader of the Bible; others hold many ideas of which I disagree. Disagreement does not mean I do not cherish their scholarship; all helped me understand the gracious disclosure of God and the history of that disclosure. Therefore, I consider them all friends.

Teachers, writers, and saints are not the only people I owe a debt of gratitude. I also am indebted to my students. For twenty-one years I have occupied the W. N. King Chair of Theology at Southern Nazarene University. In addition to this privilege, I have taught in various relationships with five other institutions of higher learning. Students not only are the recipients of my work but also are, in their own way, shapers of my thinking. Their questions, comments, and even papers have been a means of grace to me. Thank you for the honor of being your guide down the pathway of reading the Bible Christianly!

There are two other persons I would like to thank: Drs. Al Truesdale and Alex Varughese. Al was my faithful editor, and Alex is the person who invited me to undertake this writing project. Thank you, my friends.

The young people with whom I trust I have modeled faithful Bible reading best are Stephanie and Michael, my children. They have seen me with the Bible in my hands, and I hope they have seen the Word in my heart. My own children now have children. The task of faithful reading is a life-consuming charge. Deuteronomy 6:4-9 says it well:

> Hear, O Israel: The Lord is our God, the Lord alone. You shall love the Lord your God with all your heart, and with all your soul, and with all your might. Keep these words that I am commanding you today in your heart. Recite them to your children and talk about them when you are at home and when you are away, when you lie down and when you rise. Bind them as a sign on your hand, fix them as an emblem on your forehead, and write them on the doorposts of your house and on your gates.

Faithfully reading the Bible is a multigenerational journey. It takes more than a single lifetime to read the Bible well, but it is done on a day and at a time by each of us. May our children and their children catch us reading these ancient and life-giving texts. And may they interpret all of our stories as episodes in HIS.

Introduction

The author considered titling this book "Reading the Bible Christianly: A Narrative Approach to Scripture." This is an audacious title for a book on how to read the Scriptures. One might ask, "Does this author not understand the diverse ways the Bible has been read across the history of interpretation by Christians?" One can arguably say that even the early church differed on the readings of the sacred texts. What about the differences in the reading of these hallowed passages between the schools of Antioch and Alexandria? Does this author not realize that there have been Christians reading these texts for almost two millennia? The answer to these legitimate and justifiable questions is yes. Yes, this title is both overconfident and disrespectful. It is overconfident of the approach and disrespectful of all that has occurred in the history of interpretation. Nevertheless, this book is not an attempt to say that all approaches to reading Scripture have been illegitimate, but that there are too many readings of these sacred texts that are foolishly uninformed and detrimentally malformed.

As this book is being written, a great debate is being waged in the United States concerning how the Bible is used and understood. The attorney general of the United States, in defense of a White House policy on immigration, referred to Romans 13 as a warrant for Christians to accept and support the administration's policies: submit to the government. Pundits from the right and the left quoted Scripture in support of or in defiance to the attorney general's use of Scripture. Most of these persons were using the Bible for their own purposes or, as this book will eventually name them, their own narratives. Persons and communities may have various readings of events, but this does not mean that every interpretation of an event or text is accurate or even truthful. A postmodern world, the world of the early twenty-first century, is revealing the unstable condition that any interpretation of events and texts is acceptable as long as it supports the already existing belief and value system of the interpreter. Text-jacking, alternative facts, and the conviction that all beliefs are justified cry out for a book to investigate and scrutinize both the reader of texts and the texts that are read.

Are words simply sounds made by a human voice with no real connection to the way people live, or are they a part of a larger background or matrix within which all human activities find their meaning? This is the guiding query that will inform all of the investigations of this book on how to read the Bible. There is a conventional childhood chant that goes something like this: "Sticks and stones may break my bones, but words will never hurt me." Is this saying true, or are words the reason sticks and stones are used to bully, injure, and even kill people? Take for examples the prophets of the Old Testament, the disciples of Jesus, and even the Lord himself. It seems that words were used to oppress and eventually execute the Lord, his disciples, and the prophets. The good news is that words are used not only to bring about the abuse of others but also to equip the imagination of people who do scientific research, plan for the future, and even make sense of the past. Questions that need answering include the following: Where do the words used by individuals come from? How do they shape the values and intuitions of human beings? Are these values and intuitions active in people who read the Bible? And are they active in the very formation of the Bible?

Most books written on the subject of how to read the Bible go immediately to exegetical procedure and take the reader through each step of this technique. They explore the historical and literary contexts of the passage; then they help the beginning exegete understand structure and genre. Next these texts move through the analysis of words and concepts and finally to a consideration of the theological and ethical implications of a passage. If this is what the reader is looking for, then this book will cover these categories of exploration in its latter half. But before the journey is made to these important and key categories, the mystery of reading needs investigation. Reading with understanding is never simple, and it is especially difficult when one is reading an ancient text, written in a different language, with a radically different understanding of the world.

The premise of this book is threefold. First, the Bible is a collection of manuscripts that were developed across a long period, yet with precise messages that were for particular people at specific times. These messages were shaped by a combination of factors: the circumstances within which these words were spoken or written, the worldviews of the people that received these words, and the divine inspiration of these words for the specific space and time of the people to whom these words were written. The second assumption of this book is the belief that these words continue to possess the inspired/inspiring word of God disclosing his character and therefore his will for the being-saved people of God. The final presupposition is that the Bible is both stable (canonical message) and dynamic (incarnational message) in its composition and application.

Should readers of the Bible search for a stable meaning of a biblical passage, or is the significance of a text only the sense that is supplied by the reader? To answer this question of textual stability, this book will use the Bible itself to explore possible solutions. In early Christianity there was an oral text—the gospel—that was handed down by the community of believers. Evidently, the meaning of the gospel was stable enough for the apostle Paul to write these words in Galatians 1:6-9:

> I am astonished that you are so quickly deserting the one who called you in the grace of Christ and are turning to a different gospel—not that there is another gospel, but there are some who are confusing you and want to pervert the gospel of Christ. But even if we or an angel from heaven should proclaim to you a gospel contrary to what we proclaimed to you, let that one be accursed! As we have said before, so now I repeat, if anyone proclaims to you a gospel contrary to what you received, let that one be accursed!

The answer to the earlier question concerning the stability of meaning is that at least this oral text of the gospel had an unwavering substance. If this is the case for the gospel, is there a stability of meaning for the Bible as a whole? Can twenty-first-century persons know this meaning? Is this message still of great significance for contemporary persons? In order to begin to answer these questions, the ideas of French philosopher Paul Ricoeur will be used. He describes the life-changing process of understanding a sacred text as a threefold development: a precritical stage, which he calls naïveté; a critical stage, where the reader understands the worldviews involved in the texts and in reading itself; and finally, a postcritical moment, which he calls a second naïveté.[1] This threefold understanding is what this book on reading the Bible is attempting to develop for the twenty-first-century reader who craves to take the Bible seriously as sacred and authoritative for faith and practice and yet understands that it is fashioned through a long pilgrimage in time. Ricoeur's reflection on sacred texts, such as the Bible, undertakes the goal of so reading these texts with new eyes that the biblical world comes alive with its main character, God, in all of his mystery, glory and vulnerability. As the enigmatic character of God becomes discernible in the text, the reader begins to recognize that the world is none other than God's world. A second naïveté is acquired, and one's eyes are opened and ears unstopped to the footprints, fingerprints, and whispers of the unfathomable character of God. So how is it possible to read the Bible Christianly, which always means responsibly? This question demands a thoughtful response by present-day communities of faith and practice.

The Bible's long history of development and interpretation is both dynamic and stable. It is stable because it cannot mean what it never could have meant, and yet it is dynamic because its message always must be recognized and applied in a brand-new way for the people of God. This long history of composition and interpretation, as well as the history of each reader of the Bible, needs to be recognized and examined. If not, understanding a text from long ago and far away lacks stability, and the text will mean only what the reader already subconsciously believes and expects it to mean. Once a critical distance is acknowledged, then the present-day people of God have the possibility of being read by the biblical text itself. As this takes place, a new way

---

1. Paul Ricoeur, *The Symbolism of Evil*, trans. Emerson Buchanan (New York: Harper and Row, 1967), 351.

of both seeing and being in the world emerges. The goal is not an unsophisticated geocentric model of the earth, but a critical realism where worldviews are acknowledged and critically assessed. It is then that a second naïveté has the possibility of occurring, when the God whose story is narrated in the Bible is recognized in the ongoing story of the reader's "real world."

Facilitating this gift of grace compels the reader of the Bible to understand the various historical contexts of the Bible, as well as the present-day context of the reader. These historical contexts are maneuvered by worldviews that create perceptions of the way the world works, what words and concepts mean, and what is to be valued and disdained. One could say that a worldview is what a culture believes to be true about reality and how members of that culture conduct themselves in the world. All worldviews are story formed—that is, they can be narrated. This idea is not simply that each worldview has stories within it but also that it is an extended story. It is a story with a beginning and an end—a long story of a journey toward a goal, a good to be practiced. This story-formed world is also able to articulate what is wrong with the world and how this violation is overcome. Worldviews have symbols that reflect the values and derisions implied by their larger grand narratives. The performers within these narrative worlds come to an understanding of who are the good people, the heroes, and who are the bad people, the villains. These grand narratives even shape the way individuals experience and tell their own life stories. Intuitions are not neutral and similar for all people in all places and at all times. They are shaped by the stories people find themselves participating in.

To understand both the story of the Bible and the stories of readers of the Bible, this book will proceed from the analysis of story-formed worlds to the procedures of how to approach the Bible's development of its own story-formed world to finally how communities can develop an imagination equipped to participate in the story-formed world of the God to whom Scripture witnesses. In the first chapter, the reader will be introduced to the idea of multiple worldviews, which must be recognized if one is to read the Bible well. These worldviews will include the multiple linguistic worlds within the Bible and the worldview(s) of the reader. The second half of this chapter will explore how persons are formed within these linguistic worlds. This linguistic formation of persons takes place within both ancient and contemporary societies. Human beings were and are shaped by language and experience. The second chapter will explore the faith inquiry of how to understand the inspiration of Scripture in the light of the long, long development of the Bible. This chapter will outline a dynamic understanding of the formation of Scripture and inspiration. It will also examine three major ways of approaching Scripture in the light of understanding its dynamic inspiration. Does the Bible want the reader to read it as a collection of propositions, as a diary of experiences, or as a lens through which the world can be appropriated as God's world? The third chapter will ask the question, given the distinct worldviews of the ancient world, What is the Bible wanting to communicate to its readers?

For the reader who is primarily concerned with the how-to of reading the Bible, the fourth and fifth chapters will be of greatest interest. In the fourth chapter, the reader will explore how to interrogate the Scriptures. This chapter will focus on the major procedural questions involved in exegesis. The fifth chapter will investigate theological hermeneutics. Building a theological bridge between the ancient world and the present will be the focus. This chapter will explore not only how a reader can read the ancient

It is possible to read the Bible well historically and literarily but not read it well Christianly. To read the Bible Christianly, the Bible must be embodied!

passages within the Bible but also how these sacred texts can read their readers. The final chapter will consider how the Scriptures can be embodied in present-day communities and persons. It is possible to read the Bible well historically and literarily but not read it well Christianly. To read the Bible Christianly, the Bible must be embodied!

All of these investigations into how to carefully read the Bible have one purpose: for readers to be shaped by the message of the biblical witness. The hope is that little by little the readers of these sacred texts will be transformed by the mystery of the One whose story is narrated within their pages. The anticipation is that readers of these sacred texts will begin to see the world and its endowments as God's world and his grace. In the words of George Lindbeck, "the ancient practice of absorbing the universe into the biblical world" is the goal of reading the Bible Christianly.[2] When the Bible is read well, the Spirit that inspires its pages brings about the inspiration and transformation of God's treasured creation.

---

2. George Lindbeck, *The Nature of Doctrine* (Louisville, KY: Westminster John Knox Press, 1984), 135.

ONE

The Worlds We Live In

Worlds Apart

All too frequently on a Sunday morning following the pastor's sermon, parishioners say to themselves and sometimes to their pastor, "This is a very good sermon, but in the real world . . ." Does this hypothetical statement mean that the preacher's sermon is a fabrication? Hopefully not, but what it does mean is that the narrative world of the parishioner and the narrative world that the sermon arises out of are distinctive understandings of what is real. If the sermon emanates from the biblical text, then all too often the text produces the perception that it is fictitious and a misrepresentation of reality. The world of the text and the world of the parishioner seem as if they are worlds apart.

N. T. Wright writes, "When, therefore, we perceive external reality, we do so within a prior framework. That framework consists, most fundamentally, of a worldview; and worldviews . . . are characterized by, among other things, certain types of story."[1] People, all people, are story formed. What is meant by this statement is not simply that people tell stories but that they are a story. Young adults often speak

---

1. N. T. Wright, *The New Testament and the People of God*, vol. 1 of *Christian Origins and the Question of God* (Minneapolis: Fortress Press,1992), 43.

about finding themselves. What they mean is not that they are physically lost, but that they are attempting to understand a truthful story of who they are. A person's history, as it actually happened, is something that can only be grasped by telling stories about the events themselves. These events are understood from a point of view, not from some disinterested watchtower on high. They are not fabricated out of thin air, but they are an attempt to make sense of events by means of an already existing value system. An example of how this works can be seen in asking a friend, "What did you do today?" The first thing that she does is to look back across the day from a standpoint that includes a spatial, temporal, social perspective. Real events, in the light of a social-linguistic perception, will compose the story that is told of the day's activities. This story is not fiction, but perspectival. Not everything that occurred in the course of the day will be included, but only what is of value. It is the already existing system of values, purpose, and world picture that allows a person to make sense of life. When an individual becomes aware of the world picture that shapes his or her values and perspective, that person categorizes this awareness as a worldview; the same is so for a community.

Getting to know another person is the effort to make sense of his or her life story. A life story is not every occurrence that has taken place in the life of a person or a people group, but those events that are significant for understanding personal or communal identity. What is intriguing about getting to know the identity of other persons and groups is that most human beings interpret others from their own perspectives. In other words, people describe other people from their own story-formed worlds. Others are considered good or bad, right or wrong, successful or unsuccessful from the story-formed worldview of the person or community that is getting to know another. People

People of different ethnic groups, religions, and socioeconomic backgrounds understand others from their own perceptions. They tell a story of the other, even if this is not the story that the other person or community would tell.

of different ethnic groups, religions, and socioeconomic backgrounds understand others from their own perceptions. They tell a story of the other, even if this is not the story that the other person or community would tell. When a person reads the Bible, the same operation takes place. The biblical world is comprehended by the story-formed world of the reader. Therefore, it is incumbent upon all who read, especially the Bible, to recognize and attempt to understand the story-formed worlds that shape both their own life stories and the storied worlds within the Bible. Until this is at least acknowledged, a person or community is trapped in a linguistic prison.

An example of perspectival confusion can be understood from one of the aphorisms that Wittgenstein, one of the greatest philosophers of the twentieth century, pens in his *Philosophical Investigations*. He writes, "If a lion could talk, we would not understand him."[2] Many people who read this aphorism verbalize to themselves, "Of course we can understand him; he is using words that are familiar to us." Wittgenstein is not declaring that human beings cannot recognize the words used by the lion, but that the decisive meaning of the language of a lion comes from the world of lion. The lioness, if she could talk, would perceive the operations of the world in a particular way, would value and undervalue certain things in the world, and would even experience certain things or events in very different ways than do those who live in a linguistic world different from that of the lion. Wittgenstein's statement implies that lions are shaped and controlled by a world picture different from that of human beings. Lions are worlds apart from human beings, even though both inhabit the same planet.

---

2. Ludwig Wittgenstein, *Philosophical Investigations* (Oxford, UK: Basil Blackwell, 1953), 223.

What this means in reading the Bible is that there are many worldviews at work in the biblical texts and in the readers of those texts. Another Wittgenstein aphorism from *Investigations* is as follows: "A picture held us captive. And we could not get outside it, for it lay in our language and language seemed to repeat it to us inexorably."[3] World pictures are language systems. This does not mean that they are simply the surface grammar of a language such as English, where the language user understands the relationship of subjects, objects, modifiers, and verbs, but a depth of grammar where the relationships of what is believed to be real, what is to be valued, and how people live in the world are located.

What is interesting is that the Bible itself is an ongoing struggle to understand the story-formed world that is given a unique fulfillment in the person of Jesus Christ. One could say that there are worlds in conflict throughout the Scriptures. Abram (Abraham), as an old man, is called, in Genesis 12, to leave the story-formed world of the Sumerian Empire in order to become a new person, with a new name, a new story, and a new worldview. Jacob finds himself in a struggle with God within the story-formed world of promise; he emerges from this struggle as a new person named Israel. The old story of promise begins to narrate even the life of Jacob, who constantly grasps and overreaches in order to control the outcome of existence. Later in this mysterious story of God, Moses warns the people in the opening eight chapters of Deuteronomy to forsake the gods of Egypt and to reject the gods of the land that they are entering into. Even though these gods are not gods at all, they do have the power of their story, which forms a world. These story-formed worlds are filled with exemplars,

---

3. Ibid., sec. 115.

practices, symbols, values, and meaning. To pursue these gods or even to practice the Yahwistic faith in a way that other gods require would make Israel a different people, with a different story, values, and purpose. Israel would no longer be Yahweh's people because they would be living a very different story and would be shaped by a very different picture of the world.

Two of the most challenging times in ancient Israel were the Babylonian exile and later the hellenization of the world (i.e., the spread of Greek culture and influence). The Babylonian exile took place over a fifty-year period in the sixth century BC, 587-537. Israel's story seemed to fail it at a time when it needed a story-formed world the most. The symbols of Israel's identity were taken: it was ripped out of the land of promise, the house of Yahweh (the temple) was destroyed, the city of David was also obliterated, and the Davidic dynasty was demolished. How was Israel to interpret/narrate this horrific event? One possible way was to give up on its story of promise and therefore Yahweh. Another way was to believe that the stories of the majority of the world were true. These stories articulated a polytheistic world, and in that world Marduk (the Babylonian king of the gods) defeated Yahweh. A new way of narrating the old story of promise needed to be articulated. This new enunciation became a confession; it was none other than Yahweh who brought about this devastation! The people of Israel accepted this pronouncement as the judgment of their God.

The poets and storytellers of Israel were responsible for formulating this development of the plot in the story of Yahweh and his people. It should be noted that this is a dynamic turn in the plotline of Israel's story. Israel was corrupt, and injustice permeated the land of promise. Judges failed to judge rightly, and the kings failed in their leadership to enforce justice; therefore, the judge of all of the earth would judge his own people. The Babylonians and their story-formed world did not destroy Israel; they were simply a tool in the hands of Yahweh. They were a part of Israel's story, not the opposite. The story of Yahweh, narrated this way, envelops the Babylonians and the whole world. Israel's God and his story keep hope alive. If it is Yahweh who judges, then there is hope!

The story of Yahweh and his people expanded to eventually eliminate any other gods from their belief system. These inspired intuitions were already active in many of the storytellers and poets, but with exile and eventually the return of the people to the land, these theological insights were solidified. The exclusive claim of Yahweh upon his people developed into the singularity of God. Israel confessed not only Yahweh alone but also that God is one. Soon Israel's story-formed world would be narrated as follows: There is but one God who created the world and elected a people to represent him to all of creation. In the flow of history, this people became enslaved by the most powerful empire on the planet, but the Creator rescued his people from the land of Egypt and gave them a land that was promised. This land flowed with "milk and honey," and the people were to live in this blessed land as a blessing. They were given a political order that reflected the Creator's will for their life together. This Torah was to prosper and protect all of the people, but they failed to live out this political order by pursuing other gods and their alien forms of life. The result of this was a broken covenant and injustice. The Creator, their God, judged them for the purpose of making their world right and then in due course rescued them from the horror of their second bondage. This is the story that informs the second half of the book of Isaiah and the narrative world that began to configure the consciousness of Israel during the Second Temple period. What should be obvious is that the story-formed worlds are not stagnant but elastically reshaping themselves to make sense of the phenomena they encounter.

For ancient Israel, the hellenization of the world by the Greek empire was another great challenge to participating and practicing the story of Israel's God. Alexander the Great conquered the majority of the known world. A major technique of control that this empire used was to enculturate various people groups with the Greek way of life: practices, values, and institutions. The Hellenistic empires far outlasted Alexander the Great and spread Greek culture through Europe, west Asia, and northern Africa. There were two choices for response to this enculturation: embrace or resist. Hellenistic Judaism combined Jewish religious tradition with elements of Greek culture. This synergism produced great people and effects. Philo of Alexandria and even Saul of Tarsus were influenced by hellenization, and the remarkable accomplishment of hellenization was the Septuagint.[4] Two of the major centers of Hellenistic Judaism were Alexandria in northern Egypt and Antioch in southern Turkey.

Not every Jewish person or community capitulated to the appeal of Hellenism. Most of the Jews in Judea offered an obvious example of defiance to the universalizing forces of Greek culture. Those who disdained enculturation resisted the common elements of Hellenism: its language, philosophy, and art. They believed this assimilation was deeply immoral and threatening to their beliefs and form of life. Ultimately, this resistance led to a full-scale armed revolt, headed up by the family of the Maccabees, in 167-160 BC. Much of the understanding of this period can be ascertained in the intertestamental material known as the Apocrypha.

---

4. The Septuagint is the earliest extant Greek translation of the Hebrew Scriptures.

In the course of history, the Greeks gave way to the Romans, but the Roman Empire was also shaped by hellenization. First-century Judaism's responses to the merging of cultures and the empire were multifaceted and generated four major groups within Judaism: the Pharisees, the Sadducees, the Essenes, and the Zealots. Each of these groups had a way of preserving its understanding of what was required to be a faithful Jew in a time of Roman dominance. Though Judaism was diverse, it had a common narrative: it believed in one God who created the world, who elected Israel as his people, who entered into covenant with Israel and gave Israel his will in the Torah, and that the people of Israel broke the covenant with their God and each other. The differences between Judaism's four major groups can be perceived in their different interpretations of how the covenant was to be lived out.

It was into this confrontational narrative world that Jesus appeared in history. He also shared the basic story of Judaism and moreover proclaimed a message that was completely Jewish when he preached the gospel of the kingdom of God. This gospel that Jesus announced of the kingdom was anticipated by other first-century Jews, but Jesus's understanding of how God was bringing in his kingdom differed from the understandings of the other groups. Even though each of these groups shared the same initial plotline, each had a different conclusion to the story of how God would be King. As every reader knows, to change the ending of a story is to change its meaning.

With a change of meaning, there are also changes to values and practices. Hopes and dreams are comprehended and even experienced differently. Even though these five groups within first-century Judaism shared a common plotline, they were worlds apart! Jesus and his story-formed people were a threat and had to be eliminated. The other groups believed Jesus and his people to be antithetical to the purposes of Yahweh. For the other groups, the cross became the answer to what they perceived to be a malevolent embodiment of the story of Israel. In the end, the stories that other first-century Jews participated in would cry out in capitulation, "We have no king but Caesar" (John 19:15, NIV).

Perhaps this is what twenty-first-century parishioners mean when they say, "This is a very good sermon pastor, but in the real world . . ." What is understood as real is nothing less than the story-formed worlds within which each person interprets, experiences, values, and acts. The vocabulary of Christian faith is not the nucleus of the Christian language; its core is its story. When an alien story is used to read the biblical story, the reader understands the biblical story in the light of the alien story. This was the case with the syncretism with Baalism in ancient Israel, and it was the case with Hellenism toward the end of Second Temple Judaism. It was the case with the attempted reconciliation of opposing principles and practices of the Roman Empire and Christianity in the fourth century and with the creation of Christendom, and it is the same with readers today.

To read the Bible Christianly demands that readers become aware of the critical distance between themselves and the text. Reading the Bible through the lenses of race, ethnicity, nationalism, economic status, and even gender is to read the Bible for the sake of another story-formed world. The Bible is a story with a beginning and an ending. It is a story that weaves itself through history and shapes a people capable of seeing everything through its storied lens. These people value differently, because they believe differently. They come to recognize that their way of understanding everything is a new language, a new story. They believe that they are new creatures, the new humanity, born again, filled with the last-days presence of God. They constitute a new people, a royal priesthood, a holy nation. They are the new-covenant people of God, where every value is turned upside down: the last are first, leaders are servants, the poor are blessed, power is made perfect in weakness, and enemies are loved! As the Johannine community reminds the readers of its texts, the world will hate them because it hates their Lord and Savior (see John 15:18). Readers of the Christian Bible belong to a different language group, a different community; they are learning the language of the man from heaven.

Inhabiting a World

Everyday life shows itself as a world shared with other human beings. Individuals do not interpret the world apart from interaction with others. Intuitions are not unique to each person but correspond to the basic perceptions of other people who live in the same linguistic world. As an example of how this shared understanding works, a community may consider an individual to be abnormal if he or she perceives the world differently from the way the community does. Sometimes this means that the community will recognize such a person as mentally challenged or even as malevolent. At other times, the community may identify the person as special, with unique gifts. Either way, such a person is considered outside of the norm. The majority of societies do not allow divergent people to remain in the social order as if they are ordinary. Abnormal people think outside of the linguistic lines of conventional certitude.

There is no doubt that this has caused enormous pain and anguish in the history of the world. People who believe or see differently are often considered evil or ill. Communities have segregated them, burned them at the stake, locked them away in institutions, demonized and exorcized them, and even nailed them to crosses. What this means is that an individual's experience is unique to the individual, but never is it considered to be entirely private. Personal experience has a public linguistic framework. This shared framework allows persons not only to be in meaningful relationships but also to interpret their own perceptions and feelings. This framework is so embedded in the community and individual persons in that community that quite often the first place of judging actions and perceptions is in the self-talk of each individual. Guilt and pride, dread and hope, are responses of individuals to situations understood in the light of the linguistic world within which they participate. When a person is not able to self-assess, then often the community steps in to clarify, correct, or incarcerate. People who inhabit the same linguistic world bring intelligibility to individual experiences, even if the linguistic world is completely wrong about the phenomena being interpreted: the world is not flat, the sun does not revolve around the earth, and there are no witches.

What brings about this kind of exclusion of privatized experience and interpretation? It is nothing less than the linguistic worlds or grand narratives that constitute communities of memory. Everyone participates in a linguistic community, with its values, symbols, and practices. The meanings that are given to everything are located in these linguistic communities with their narrative worldviews. In other words, languages and value systems are manifestations of particular communities of memory and do not exist outside of the social imagery in which they are used.

It is important to understand how people are habituated into a particular worldview with its beliefs and values. It is also vital to examine how the conversion of individuals and even communities takes place. In order to explore these themes, the reader needs to be mindful of a few questions: What does it mean to be a particular kind of person? How is character formed? How are persons enculturated into a particular linguistic world? And how and why does transformation take place with persons and communities?

Persons become a part of a particular community of memory and share its narrative worldview principally because they are born into this relational network. These systems are much more than simply arrangements of defense and care. They are structures that bring organization and classification to beliefs, values, and desires. They allow persons to perceive, understand, aspire, and dread. These networks are linguistic! Perhaps one could describe them as W. V. O. Quine does as "web[s]-of-belief."[5] They are not only places where answers are found, but they form the background of human questioning and judging. Wittgenstein writes in *On Certainty*, "I did not get my picture of the world by satisfying myself of its correctness; nor do I have it because I am satisfied of its correctness. No: it is the inherited background against which I distinguish between true and false."[6] He also writes in *Culture and Value*, "Perhaps what is inexpressible (what I find mysterious and am not able to express) is the background against which whatever I could express has its meaning."[7]

Individuals enact the linguistic worlds they are born into because they observe the performance of exemplars, participate in communal practices, hear stories that reinforce some aspect of these worlds, and adhere to symbols that mediate the values of these story-formed worlds. The beliefs and values of these linguistic frameworks have an

---

5. W. V. O. Quine and J. S. Ullian, *The Web of Belief* (New York: McGraw-Hill, 1970).

6. Ludwig Wittgenstein, *On Certainty*, ed. G. E. M. Anscombe and G. H. von Wright, trans. Denis Paul and G. E. M. Anscombe (New York: Basil Blackwell, 1969), sec. 94.

7. Ludwig Wittgenstein, *Culture and Value*, trans. P. Winch (Oxford: Basil Blackwell, 1980), 16.

underlying grand narrative that gives an interpretation of where reality comes from and where it is going, its ultimate meaning and worth. As individuals participate in a narrative world, they come to recognize the story of their own lives in its light. Understanding oneself as a success or failure, a hero or a villain, a saint or a sinner, is determined by the way one's own life is identified in the light of the larger narrative. This understanding of the self is what shapes the ethical life: how one sees, acts, and even feels in the world. People do what seems natural to them, and what seems natural to them is the story-formed world they participate in.

Concrete examples of this can be described in the way racial and gender perceptions take place for communities. When toddlers of racially and ethnically diverse groups are placed in a room together, they do not discriminate based upon the color of their skin or even gender. They may grab the toys of other toddlers, but they do not do this based upon ethnicity. Something happens to these toddlers as they become language users in the course of their lives; they become biased based upon a variety of factors. These factors include the families that raise these children, the institutions they participate in, and the media they are exposed to. In other words, the stories that they are told by family, friends, and their culture; the exemplars, considered both good and bad, that they observe; and the practices that habituate them through the institutions that bring order to their social context will shape the point of view of these toddlers becoming adults. If a person grows up in a very racist family, with racist friends and no exposure to people who are racially different, hearing racist stories, the chances are very probable that this individual will be a racist. People are habituated into a way of life with all of its beliefs and values.

The perspectives of the writers and early readers of the Scriptures were shaped by the intersection of the existing worldviews that they participated in, by events that were taking place in and around the times they were writing and reading, and by the inspiration of God upon their lives.

What this means for reading the Bible is that people who are racist or misogynistic will understand passages of Scripture differently than will people who have been shaped in a linguistic community that values people of different races, ethnicities, or genders. If a person is raised in a linguistic community that is very prejudice against women, then that person will read texts such as 1 Corinthians 14:34 as a validation of their point of view: "Women should be silent in the churches. For they are not permitted to speak, but should be subordinate, as the law also says." Such a person will also disregard the baptismal assumption that Paul uses in Galatians 3:28: "There is no longer Jew or Greek, there is no longer slave or free, there is no longer male and female; for all of you are one in Christ Jesus." These selective ways of reading will not necessarily be deliberate on the part of the reader, but it will seem natural to focus on one text and ignore the implications of the other.

What this also means about reading the Bible is that the perspectives of the writers and early readers of the Scriptures were shaped by the intersection of the existing worldviews that they participated in, by events that were taking place in and around the times they were writing and reading, and by the inspiration of God upon their lives. The inspiration of God's Spirit upon the writers and readers of the Bible took place in the world they participated in. Worldviews and historical events were not eliminated because of the inspiring activity of God. For example, early Christians believed that they were entering through baptism into a new reality with its own values and social categories. This new reality is the kingdom of God, which was announced and embodied by Jesus, inaugurated by his crucifixion and resurrection, and enabled by the outpouring of the Holy Spirit. Therefore, they understood that they were raised in newness of life and that their citizenship and language were regulated by the man from heaven.

It is important for the interpreter of Scripture to be continually aware of both the perspectives of the modern-day readers and the perspectives of the writers and ancient readers. Perspectivalism is not an opinion, but a form of life. In other words, the way a person sees and understands the world and the events within it is shaped by the milieu of communal life. When the communal activities are examined historically, they reveal a collective way of performing or living in the world. One might say that communities of memory are what they practice. These socially embodied narratives habituate the convictions and values of those who participate in them. The conflicts between narrative worlds are obvious within the Bible: Abram (Abraham) and the Sumerian Empire, Moses and the Egyptian Empire, Baalism and the story of Yahweh, and many other conflictual narrative worlds. Worlds in conflict are obvious between Jesus and the Judaism of his day and between Paul and the "men from Jerusalem" (see Acts 15; Gal. 2). Twenty-first-century readers are also participants in story-formed worlds. If the reader of Scripture is not aware of these various narratives and their embodied ways of living, then the reader will be imprisoned by these worlds.

Perhaps the question for anyone who is beginning to realize the implications of a habituating form of life is, How is it possible to choose a different worldview? What would be the motivation or desire to pursue a different way of believing and valuing? Perhaps the answer to this question is that no one on his or her own can choose a different set of beliefs and values. It takes a miracle from outside of an individual to bring about a crisis that begins the process of transformation. Christians call this miracle the work of God's grace. The question is, How does this transformation begin? There are many examples in the Scriptures of how this conversion takes place, with most of these examples sharing some sort of family resemblance with one another. For the purposes of this chapter, three instances in the Bible that describe this alteration of linguistic worlds will be explored: the call of the prophet in Isaiah 6, the Damascus road experience of Saul of Tarsus, and Jesus's conversation with Nicodemus in John 3.

Isaiah 6 is a vision of the mystery of God's manifestation: the prophet sees God. This vision takes place during a time of great crisis, "the year that King Uzziah died" (v. 1), which was a period of disorientation for Judah. It was in the midst of this revelatory event that the prophet comes to realize his own orientation toward reality, "I am a man of unclean lips, and I live among a people of unclean lips; yet my eyes have seen the King, the LORD of hosts!" (v. 5). What is of great importance for the reader of this vision is that the prophet acknowledges his inability to operate within the linguistic understanding of the divine King he has just seen.

This realization of uncleanness also includes his linguistic community. They share the same fate of "Woe!" Divine grace not only initiates this conceptual change for the prophet but also calls the prophet to the work of being a divine messenger to the people. What is fascinating is that Isaiah is told that his message will fail. The natural response to this news of failure is, "How long?" (v. 11). Yahweh gives what seems on the surface to be a cryptic reply:

Until cities lie waste
without inhabitant,
and houses without people,
and the land is utterly desolate;
until the LORD sends everyone far away,
and vast is the emptiness in the midst of the land.
Even if a tenth part remain in it,

> it will be burned again,
> like a terebinth or an oak
>> whose stump remains standing
>> when it is felled. (Vv. 11-13)

What can this reply possibly mean? Perhaps there are many implications to this judgment oracle, but this much is for sure, it is a description of an epistemological crisis.[8] Because of Judah's destruction, its old way of knowing and being in the world no longer is able to account for the phenomenon of the community's existence. A new way of perceiving is necessary, and this new way is understood in this oracle as a purification that orients the community toward the divine life. The remains of the community are considered the "holy seed" (v. 13). The destruction of the people suggests that only disorientation allows for the possibility of a new orientation. The structures and symbols of the old way of living are destroyed. It is out of utter befuddlement that a new way of knowing and being is possible: "The holy seed is its stump" (v. 13). Israel will reflect the Holy One, which at least means that they will share in the Holy One's conceptual point of view. Isaiah does not believe that the people will be omniscient, but they will share in "the knowledge of the LORD" (11:9). Because the Holy One is none other than the creator of the world, this new orientation of God's people will correspond to the way reality is created to function.

A second description of an epistemological transformation is taken from the Damascus road experience of Saul of Tarsus. Acts 9 describes the event of Saul traveling toward Damascus to threaten the people of the Way. As he journeyed toward the area, a light from heaven struck him

---

8. An epistemological crisis is a turning point in the way that a person or a community understands or knows something to be real or of value.

down and blinded him. In this state of disorientation Saul was confronted by both the divine voice of the exalted Lord and eventually his servant Ananias. This disorientation and reorientation describe the phenomenon of seeing and interpreting reality in radically new ways. Saul is transformed into Paul with a new language, the language of the man from heaven (1 Cor. 15:47-49). Paul believes that those who are transformed will bear the "image of the man of heaven" (v. 49), which at least means that they will share his values and language. It is impossible to experience this newness of life without bearing witness to this new life. Old ways of seeing, believing, and valuing have passed away; all things have become new (2 Cor. 5:17). To be a new creature is to have a language that is able to narrate both the new life and the old life in the light of the new understanding.

A third description of this linguistic transformation is discovered in Jesus's conversation with Nicodemus in John 3. In this passage Nicodemus, a Pharisee, comes to Jesus by night and addresses him as "Rabbi, . . . who has come from God" (v. 2). Jesus immediately responds to Nicodemus by saying, "No one can see the kingdom of God without being born from above" (v. 3). The kingdom of God, being born again, and awareness are brought into a synergistic relationship in this passage. This Johannine statement of new birth corresponds to Paul's conception of newness of life. To "see" in this context is to discern and experience the new reality that God is creating. This new existence is given from "above," the place and perspective of God. Again, it should be noticed that a new orientation is necessary to perceive the kingdom of God. The mystery of this new orientation is the inspiration and creativity of God's own Spirit. The disorientation of Nicodemus in this conversation is a reminder that old ways of perceiving do not comprehend the new way that God is creating.

What do these three passages of Scripture have in common when it comes to the transformation of linguistic worlds? First, a new orientation is possible only when an old orientation is challenged and eventually removed. The elimination of an old way of perceiving is usually brought about by an epistemological crisis, some phenomenon that challenges old ways of interpreting and understanding. In Isaiah's vision it was the loss of the king, who was the security of the nation, that allowed for the real king to be seen high and lifted up. In Saul's experience, it was his blindness that brought the soon-to-be apostle to a place where he could see the ascended Lord. In the encounter with Nicodemus, it was his utter confusion about becoming born again that brought on his crisis in understanding. A new way of knowing is possible only when an old way of knowing is challenged. This challenge is brought on in the three texts by the inability to narrate the phenomena with the old story-formed worlds. A phenomenon must either be interpreted by the longstanding narrative framework of a person or community, or the phenomenon will create an epistemological crisis that will reshape the old framework into something new. Jesus says it this way, "Neither is new wine put into old wineskins; otherwise, the skins burst, and the wine is spilled, and the skins are destroyed; but new wine is put into fresh wineskins, and so both are preserved" (Matt. 9:17).

A second commonality of these passages is that a new narrative understanding is introduced. This new narrative includes both the ability to interpret the phenomenon that causes the epistemological crisis and also the ability to narrate the old narrative understanding in the light of the new. Isaiah was not only able to see God as the King "high and lifted up" (Isa. 6:1, KJV) but also to understand himself and Israel as "a people of unclean lips" (v. 5). Saul was able not only to hear the exalted Lord but also to narrate his old life as a persecutor of the church. The Nicodemus encounter was able to reorient the reader of John to the reality of life in the kingdom. It also enabled the reader to narrate life outside of the kingdom as the old decaying way of humanity.

Converts to early Christianity went through a process in their attempt to learn the language that would allow them to interpret and experience the world differently. George Lindbeck describes this when he writes the following:

> Pagan converts to the catholic mainstream . . . were first attracted by the Christian community and form of life. The reasons for attraction ranged from the noble to the ignoble and were as diverse as the individuals involved; but for whatever motives, they submitted themselves to prolonged catechetical instruction in which they practiced new modes of behavior and learned the stories of Israel and their fulfillment in Christ. Only after they had acquired proficiency in the alien Christian language and form of life were they deemed able intelligently to profess the faith, to be baptized.[9]

In all of these cases the old is understood in the light of the new.

A new way of perceiving the world is not something that is easy for individuals or communities to experience, much less accept. If something has always been interpreted one way, then to be told it is another seems like nonsense to anyone who is held captive by a particular conceptual picture. It is only when a person or community is enabled to interpret the phenomenon differently that a new lens to understand the world becomes a reality. In this dawning, the old way of seeing is still recognized and understood as a former way of

---

9. Lindbeck, *Nature of Doctrine*, 132.

interpreting the world and phenomena in that world, but it is done from the vantage point of the emergence of a new way to interpret the phenomena. The tendency for most communities and individuals is to hold tightly to the established ways of believing and interpreting the world. Transformation is not as simple as saying to oneself, "I'm going to change my way of understanding the world."

TWO

God Leads His Children Along

The story-formed world of Israel's God was developed over a very long period, with diverse perspectives on how to exactly tell and embody the story. By the first century AD though, the story line was narrated in parallel ways by the majority of factions in Judaism, but as noted in chapter 1, each group's understanding of how the story would end seemed different. These diverse groups—Pharisees, Sadducees, Essenes, and Zealots—developed their own separate conclusions for this anticipated end. These various ways of understanding the end or goal of Israel's story altered its meaning and shaped each group's convictions, practices, and values. With these alternative ways of understanding the culmination of the story came different ways of interpreting and participating in the world. Again, as observed earlier, the conclusion of a story regulates what kind of tale is being told.

So how does this narrative world of God develop? By the first century AD Israel shared a common plotline: There is one God who created everything that exists. This one Creator elected Israel to be his people with the purpose of bearing witness to his character and will for the rest of creation. In order for his people to know and practice his will, he assisted them through various gifts: the rescue from Egyptian bondage, the giving of Torah, and the bestowal of the land are some of these gifts. The story that Israel tells itself includes its failure to observe the will of God in the land and, in so doing, its pollution of this holy gift. The people were no longer capable of dwelling in the land, so by an act of God's judgment, they were removed. Exile lasted only long enough, fifty years, for the people to remember who they were. This led to a repentance of the people and their return and restoration. What seemed like a second exodus was none other than the hand of their God liberating and reestablishing his people once again in the land. The vision of what Israel would be as God's witness and blessing never completely materialized for the Second Temple Jews, and there was an anticipation of a further and comprehensive fulfillment of the grand vision of God's will and reign for Israel and all of creation.

This Jewish story of God continues to unfold with many further episodes, but its basic plotline remains as the enduring story line of the narrative. It was into this story, with its various endings, that Jesus arrives telling and embodying the same plotline with his own interpretation of its completion. His interpretation of the story called for a reshaping of many of the practices and values of first-century Judaism. As a reader of the New Testament knows, Jesus and his conclusion to Israel's story of God were rejected by all of the major groups of first-century Israel.

This book on how to read the Bible has argued that the Bible is the story of God told from a point of view or, possibly more correctly, points of view. A point of view is always established by a world picture, which also yields a belief and value system. People only believe in what they understand to be true, and people only value what they believe is real. No adults in Western culture believe in unicorns, fairies, and leprechauns, yet they may tell stories of these creatures to their young children. The telling of these stories is for some other purpose than describing what a human

Human beings narrate history from a point of view. Therefore, events are recognized and understood differently with a newly acquired set of beliefs and values.

being is to believe. The proof of this statement can be seen in the way financial concerns are engaged by these adult storytellers. These narrators do not risk their own fortunes or lives in search of a leprechaun's pot of gold. In other words, adult storytellers believe these characters belong to the world of fiction. When a child moves from the domain of unicorns, leprechauns, and fairies, his or her world changes. The child values differently and even sees the universe in a different way. The same goes for communities of memory when they begin to believe differently about what is real. Shifting worldviews are always extremely difficult for cultures. A social order resists these shifts because they change the way the world is understood, valued, and even experienced. A worldview conversion challenges not only a group's way of experiencing the cosmos but also its way of remembering events.

Human beings narrate history from a point of view. Therefore, events are recognized and understood differently with a newly acquired set of beliefs and values. The past is always narrated perspectivally, with new convictions about what is to be pursued and with different considerations about who are the heroes and the villains. Examples of this can be seen in the way American history is narrated by different people groups. When history is written from an African American or Native American perspective, it has different considerations about what determines the good that history is pursuing. Heroes and villains are also determined very differently than they are when history is written from the vantage point of a white European descendant. One who is seen as a rebel from one narration is seen as a freedom fighter from another. From one narration, a person can read that the rights of a slave owner are deprived when a slave is assisted by the Underground Railroad's network of secret routes and safe houses; from another, the rights of a human being are granted when a slave is liberated through the help of the Railroad to reach the Free States and Canada. Perspective determines the meaning of a historical narrative, and perspective belongs to a worldview.

What are the shared convictions (and therefore the perspective) of the biblical story? Ancient Jews would answer this question by confessing that God acts in history and in creation and that he entrusts traces of his presence in both time (history) and space (creation) to his people. This answer assumes a theological category called revelation. So how does revelation operate? And in what way does it correspond to the formation of what today is called the Bible? The remainder of this chapter will attempt to answer these two questions and ask a third: How does the Bible, which is considered inspired, need to be read in the light of the answers given to the first two questions?

Revelation and the Formation of the Bible

Every text in the Old Testament, Apocrypha,[1] and New Testament emerged from a particular social, political, and cultural environment over the course of many centu-

---

1. The Hebrew Bible is considered complete with the oracles of Malachi. After this period of time, 450 BC through AD 50, many documents were written and circulated throughout the Jewish synagogues and early gatherings of the followers of the resurrected Christ. Some of these documents gradually came to be regarded by some believers as Scripture. Many early Christians regarded them as valuable for reading and edification, and in some editions of the Bible, they were interspersed among the Old Testament books. There are fourteen books that make up this collection in many Bibles today. Martin Luther, in his Bible translation of 1534, removed the apocryphal books from their usual places in the Old Testament and placed them at the end of the Old Testament. After that, many Protestant Bibles omitted them completely. The Roman Catholic Council of Trent, in 1546, explicitly enumerated the apocryphal books approved by the Roman Catholic Church as inspired, and they are always included in the Roman Catholic Bibles and are interspersed among the books of the Old Testament. These books are at least helpful in understanding the traditioning process of this period and how it informed the major Jewish groups of the first century AD.

ries. This means that every text represents a worldview and sometimes various worldviews as the text develops through time. The purpose of using various critical methods, in interpreting the Scripture, is to understand the events that interact with the biblical texts as well as the worldviews of these different periods of time. The methodological classification that forms the umbrella of these various approaches is called historical criticism. It endeavors to explore the assorted origins of the biblical writings and trace their development within their distinctive historical contexts.

The deposit of Israel's faith, as recorded in the Scriptures, conveys theological reflections upon various events. In other words, these ancient Jewish people understood their own history as taking place within the unfolding of the story of their God. But how is a reader of the Bible to understand this masterful narrative's development? There seems to be at least several stages in the development of this confessional process of the formation of Scripture: the incident that takes place, a theological disclosure of the meaning of the event, the oral process of remembering the event in the light of its theological confession, the gathering of various stories orally that begin to form subplots in the developing story of God, the process of transcribing these oral confessions, the gathering together of various writings, the authority given to these writings as Scripture, and finally the long, long process of establishing the canon.

The defining event in Israel's memory is the miraculous escape from Egyptian bondage. This event was the culmination of a variety of events called the plagues. Something happened, but what does it mean? All events, even this communal identity-forming event of the exodus, are meaningful only because language provides that meaning. The great confession located in Deuteronomy 26:8 says, "The LORD brought us out of Egypt with a mighty hand and an outstretched arm, with a terrifying display of power, and with signs and wonders." The language that was available for these Hebrew slaves of long ago was a language that allowed them to confess that a god, named Yahweh, was responsible for the event.

Other language users, the Egyptians, understood a different cause for these phenomena in nature. Exodus 7:20-24 records the response to the first plague:

> Moses and Aaron did just as the LORD commanded. In the sight of Pharaoh and of his officials he lifted up the staff and struck the water in the river, and all the water in the river was turned into blood, and the fish in the river died. The river stank so that the Egyptians could not drink its water, and there was blood throughout the whole land of Egypt. But the magicians of Egypt did the same by their secret arts; so Pharaoh's heart remained hardened, and he would not listen to them, as the LORD had said. Pharaoh turned and went into his house, and he did not take even this to heart. And all the Egyptians had to dig along the Nile for water to drink, for they could not drink the water of the river.

This is but one of many examples in the exodus story that points to multiple interpretations of events. Every time an event is described, the portrayal is a confession of faith. This declaration is the meaning that is given to an occurrence based upon a larger belief system. Only the categories that are already in a language and its worldview are available for a person to articulate what has taken place. Therefore, the language that is used to bring meaning to any event, both ancient and modern, is a confession of the language user. This means two things: individuals are dependent upon a community of memory for the conceptual categories to interpret an event, and they share common beliefs with these same language users. Conceptual categories develop in connection with the beliefs of a narrated worldview. A person cannot confess what he or she does not believe, and a person cannot believe when he or she does not have an adequate conceptual category.

A very important question needs to be asked in this argument: Where did this group of ragtag slaves develop the conceptual categories to recognize the hand of Yahweh in the plagues and deliverance from Egypt? Very likely the many slaves in ancient Egypt were multifarious and included more than the descendants of Jacob. They were at least an assortment of Semitic people groups and perhaps other ethnic groups as well. Egypt, in antiquity, was known as the breadbasket of the world. The annual flooding of the Nile produced rich harvests, and when famine hit neighboring lands, starving groups of people often made their way to the fruitful land of Egypt. This is the reason that the Bible gives for Jacob and his clan coming to Egypt, and it is most probably the reason many other groups of people came to Egypt as well. Like Joseph, there were also people who were sold into slavery and brought to Egypt. Other slaves were captured in battles and pressed into slavery. So, where does the conceptual framework that allows for this confession come from? These slaves were not univocal as language users. They would have arrived in Egypt with a diversity of worldviews at different times.

Slavery, over many generations, takes intellectual imagination out of circulation. In other words, slaves do not have the prospect of education. Genesis 15:13 implies that Abraham's descendants would be in Egypt for 400 years, and Exodus 12:40-41 states that they were there for 430 years. This does not mean that the descendants of Jacob were slaves the entire time, but the implication in the story of Yahweh and his people is that they were slaves for a very long time. To be a slave meant that a person was but a cog in the economic machine of Egypt. Slaves were not given the status of being fully human. They did not have a day off, as the Sabbath commandment in Deuteronomy 5:12-15 states. They were expendable to the point that when they became a threat because of their numbers, they were thinned out like a pack of wild animals. This is what the opening of the story of Moses is describing in the book of Exodus. The implication is that these slaves, who were increasing in number, were illiterate and did not have the time or resources for educational or cultic practices. How do people without time, resources, and training develop the conceptual categories necessary to interpret the events of their world as the hand of Yahweh?

Possibly, a few of the descendants of Jacob kept alive some of the stories of the patriarchs. The stories of election and promise, which would be difficult for the people to imagine across centuries of generational slavery, were kept alive by passing these stories down from one generation to another. These stories would conceivably become the stories of other Semitic people groups, who were also slaves, in the progression of time. Stories of Abraham, Isaac, and Jacob were conceivably the identity stories that began to provide the interpretive categories needed to confess that Yahweh brought us out of Egypt! Moses was told as much when he was commissioned by Yahweh from the burning bush. Exodus 3:6 states, "I am the God of your father, the God of Abraham, the God of Isaac, and the God of Jacob." The inference is that Moses was told the stories of the patriarchs by someone.

Clearly, as this example implies, these stories were preserved and passed on orally. This does not mean that every word was memorized, but the stories became a part of the family and clan storytelling. Storytelling was prominent in the ancient world. No one knows when the first story was actually told, but one thing is for sure, before human beings were able to write, they had to rely on their memory to learn anything. Good storytellers were esteemed. They provided information and formation, and they were an aspect of entertainment. As families grouped with other families and formed clans, the storyteller, who was good at narrating heroic events or other important occasions of the tribe, began to attain a position of respect and power. People found storytellers interesting and were captured by every twist and turn in their accounts. These stories were also shared with others in faraway locations when people traveled. The stories traveled with the storytellers, and when they returned home, they brought with them new tales of exceptional places and people.

Individual stories were collected and grouped together orally across time. The groupings of these stories developed into various episodes in a larger story. Most likely the stories of Abraham, Isaac, and Jacob were not originally one continuous story, but various stories brought together into a somewhat coherent plotted sequence. The same can be said concerning the stories of the judges and the kings and even the stories of Jesus. This does not mean that these stories are fictive, but it does suggest that the identity-forming narratives were gathered and told in such a way that a coherent narrative began to develop. This emerging and expanding of a narrative took place over an extended period, most probably generations.

Eventually some of these stories, genealogies, laws, and poems were written down. What could possibly influence a group of people who lived in an oral tradition to write down parts of that oral tradition? The answer to this question is multidimensional: some of the erudite portions were originally written material, some of the stories and poems were told in diversified ways and therefore necessitated an invariable statement, but also people began to forget these stories and poems. With the loss of the stories and poems came a loss of communal identity, and with the loss of communal identity came a loss of beliefs and values. Deuteronomy makes this point often by reminding its readers not to forget the story of God:

> When the LORD your God has brought you into the land that he swore to your ancestors, to Abraham, to Isaac, and to Jacob, to give you—a land with fine, large cities that you did not build, houses filled with all sorts of goods that you did not fill, hewn cisterns that you did not hew, vineyards and olive groves that you did not plant—and when you have eaten your fill, take care that you do not forget the LORD, who brought you out of the land of Egypt, out of the house of slavery. (6:10-12)

To remember God is to remember his story.

Besides the gathering together of stories orally, the people of God began to gather together written stories and even episodes that eventually became a larger literary composite. The stories of a particular people group shaped that group's perspective, beliefs, and values in its larger social context. There was always an oral framework within which written documents found their linguistic home. In biblical studies the analysis of the oral and written development of these documents is referred to as tradition criticism. The purpose of this procedure is to understand the process of development that occurs within the ongoing influences of time. Biblical texts did not fall from the sky. Source criticism is another method used to differentiate the various literary strands in the canonical texts themselves. Examples of these various written sources can be discovered in the diverse literary strands of both the Pentateuch and the Synoptic Gospels.

Scholars for many years have had different assumptions on what basis and how the literary strands in the Pentateuch are understood and were developed. One hypothesis is that the Pentateuch is composed of four sources, each originally a separate and independent document. This understanding holds that they were joined together at various points in time by a series of redactors. Another suggestion is that the Torah is composed of a collection of small fragments. This also is understood to have taken place across a long period. A third assumption is that there is a single core document supplemented by fragments taken from many sources across time. What each of these theories has in common are the obvious literary distinctions in style and vocabulary that are evident in the canonical text itself. As stated earlier, the Synoptic Gospels are also best understood as being composed of various written and some oral sources. Again, the Bible did not fall from the sky or even from a single pen, but eventually the books themselves began to form as a complete unit.

In time these collections of literary texts began to have the authority of Scripture. It is difficult to discern when the various portions of the Bible were acknowledged as Scripture. What is probable is that different subgroups in Israel acknowledged certain laws, poems, and stories as Scripture before other subgroups acknowledged the same texts. In 622 BC the book of the law was found in the Jerusalem temple. This discovery was the basis of a reform enacted by King Josiah for the nation. This law code was perhaps one of the earliest expressions of what could be classified as Scripture. It had authority! Many scholars believe that some portion of Deuteronomy 12–26 made up this law code. The reform was Deuteronomic because it consisted of removing pagan altars and idols and destroying rural sanctuaries and moved toward a centralizing of worship at the Jerusalem temple. This is clearly Deuteronomic theology. Scripture, as a concept, has an authorization to regulate the way a people believe and participate in their community.

By stating that these texts are Scripture, it means they have a certainty of conviction in matters of faith and practice for the communities that embrace them. Second Timothy 3:16-17 states, "All scripture is inspired by God and is useful for teaching, for reproof, for correction, and for training in righteousness, so that everyone who belongs to God may be proficient, equipped for every good work." The author of 2 Timothy did not understand his own writing as Scripture, but he would have at least understood the Scriptures to include the Law and the Prophets. This is also what Jesus implies by his saying in Matthew 5:17-19:

> Do not think that I have come to abolish the law or the prophets; I have come not to abolish but to fulfill. For truly I tell you, until heaven and earth pass away, not one letter, not one stroke of a letter, will pass from the law until all is accomplished. Therefore, whoever breaks one of the least of these commandments, and teaches others to do the same, will be called least in the kingdom of heaven; but whoever does them and teaches them will be called great in the kingdom of heaven.

What is considered sacred writings for one religion, or even a subgroup within a religion, is not necessarily considered sacred writings for another. The formation of Scripture is a long and involved matter for the people of faith.

One final phase takes place in this intricate development of the Bible, the canonical process. The English word "canon" comes from a Greek word that means "rule" or "measuring stick." This process consists of at least four major moments in the development of an official list of books

If the community claims that the Bible is inspired and yet lives from an alternative narrative (with its beliefs, practices, and values), the words of the Bible appear empty and without the power to shape reality.

that the Judeo-Christian religious community regards as authoritative Scripture. These historical moments are the canonization of the Torah, the canonization of the Prophets, the canonization of the Writings, and the canonization of the New Testament. It should also be remembered that other books were a part of the official canon of Christian Scripture and that great debate on what should be included in the Christian canon took place all the way up to and through the Reformation.

If the above description of the formation of the Bible is to some degree accurate, then in what ways can the community of faith understand the inspiration of Scripture? For example, does God cause or enable the events that the story describes, and/or does God inspire the first confessors of these events who provide meaning for the incidents themselves? If God does inspire the first confessors, is this confession in the light of the worldview that the confessor participates in or does God impose a different worldview altogether? Another possibility is that God breathed the words that are finally written down in the Bible and that have made their way into the twenty-first century. Perhaps this would mean that only the canon is inspired, not the events or progression of its formation. Even though human beings are unable to know exactly how or what God has breathed into the Bible, what needs to be acknowledged is that when persons confess the Scriptures are inspired, that confession is itself a matter of faith. There is no neutral evidence that can convince a nonbeliever that the Bible is in fact inspired. To say the Bible is inspired by God is a confession of the community's faith.

So why do people believe that the Bible is inspired? The answer is multidimensional: the first two answers given are cultural and philosophical; the final answer is a confession of faith. First, those who believe participate in a community that trusts, values, and practices the reading of Scripture. What is meant by this statement is that the language of the community of faith shapes the beliefs and form of life of those who confess that the Bible is inspired. If the community claims that the Bible is inspired and yet lives from an alternative narrative (with its beliefs, practices, and values), the words of the Bible appear empty and without the power to shape reality. These words of confession have the possibility of believability only when they function as an authority for the community of people who bear witness to them in their form of life. Inspired must at least include inspiring those who make the confession if there is to be a believability by those outside the faith and even those who are attempting to practice the faith.

Second, the Bible becomes a lens through which the Bible's readers interpret the world and its history. This is the way all linguistic frameworks operate. Perspective, the way of interpreting and participating in the world, is always contextual. For communities that believe the Bible reveals the mystery of God, the world is understood as his world. A typological analysis of the Bible allows its readers to interpret phenomena through the pattern of the ongoing story of God. This story, in all of its multiplicity, becomes a paradigm for interpreting all existence as God's gift. When incidents are interpreted through this lens, then the conclusion is that experience itself validates the witness of Scripture.

Finally and most importantly, readers are given the gift of God's Spirit to enable faith in and the practice of the biblical story. Only God can open the eyes and ears of humanity to perceive his fingerprints and overhear his whispers in the unfolding of history. To trust that the Bible is inspired by God is a gift of God's grace to the believer.

When one looks at the long history of the formation of the Bible, the church and this author believe that God was and is inspiring the entire process of its development. The connotation is that God instigated the events recorded in the Bible's narrative, God stirred the confessors to interpret the phenomena as his acts in history, God motivated the community to pass on these declarations of faith in oral and written form, God assisted his people so that they acknowledged the authority of the texts as Scripture, and finally God asserted his noncoercive will in the entire process of canonical authorization. It is also conceivable that God continues to breathe through these ancient words his own Word. This ongoing movement of God is the premise that is operational in this book on how to read the Bible.

Perhaps, even with the closed canon of Scripture, God continues to speak through the words of the Bible his dynamic Word of self-disclosure to his people today! God continues to lead his children along. When the people of faith describe preaching, they are not implying that it is merely a religious speech or even ethical instruction. The Christian church believes that preaching is the proclamation of the Word of God. God's Word is not simply a collection of printed words in a book, but the very consciousness and language of the Creator-Redeemer. God's Word was in the beginning, "and the Word was with God, and the Word was God. He was in the beginning with God. All things came into being through him, and without him not one thing came into being. What has come into being in him was life, and the life was the light of all people. . . . And the Word became flesh and lived among us, and we have seen his glory, the glory as of a father's only son, full of grace and truth" (John 1:1-4, 14).

God's Word creates, and it is finally displayed so that its hearing is made visible in flesh and blood. The early church did not doubt what the Word of God sounds like; it

sounds like the form of life incarnate in the person of Jesus
Christ. First John 1:1-3 confesses,

> We declare to you what was from the beginning, what we
> have heard, what we have seen with our eyes, what we
> have looked at and touched with our hands, concerning
> the word of life—this life was revealed, and we have seen
> it and testify to it, and declare to you the eternal life that
> was with the Father and was revealed to us—we declare
> to you what we have seen and heard so that you also may
> have fellowship with us; and truly our fellowship is with
> the Father and with his Son Jesus Christ.

Does this discussion concerning the breath of God
in the Scriptures mean that the words of the Bible can be
decontextualized and applied directly to the inhabitants
of the present-day world? The answer to this is no. If the
ultimate revelation of God in Christ conveys anything, it
is that God discloses Godself in incarnational ways. To be
incarnational is to be contextual in space and time. This is
what it means for God to reveal Godself to humanity: God
empties Godself to meet creatures where they are (Phil. 2:5-
11). It seems terribly naïve to believe that the Creator had
to teach physics, cosmology, and philosophy before disclosing Godself to people who occupied a worldview different
from the worldview of modern science today. It also seems
incredibly naïve to believe that the present worldview will
be the same worldview in the forty-first century. Implied
in this statement is that when God speaks and acts in the
world, God does so in ways that make sense to people in
the space and time that they occupy. The Bible will be no
more obsolete two thousand years from now than it was a
thousand years ago or is today.

How Does the Bible Need to Be Read?

In the light of what has been said about the inspiration of Scripture and the worldviews that are reflected in the Bible itself, what is the most appropriate way for the community of faith to approach the reading and application of the Bible? In his seminal book *The Nature of Doctrine*, George Lindbeck describes three major methodological categories to practice the craft of theology.[2] He gives these three approaches the following labels: cognitive-propositional, experiential-expressive, and cultural-linguistic. The remainder of this chapter will explore these three methodological approaches in their application to reading the Bible.

A cognitive-propositional approach to theology implies that a theological statement pictures an exact state of affairs. Therefore, a propositional statement is either true or false and can be lifted out of its original context and placed into any other context as a truth statement. For example, if "a doctrine is once true, it is always true, and if it is once false, it is always false."[3] When this approach is used in reading the Bible, it indicates that a single assertion in the Scriptures is either true or false as a reality in the universe. The biblical statement is not context dependent for interpretation, for the world is as it is pictured in the statement. For a person who approaches Scripture from the perspective of propositional thinking, a biblical statement will have the same truth value today as it had in the first century and as it had in the thirteenth century BC.

A proposition is true only if it is true at all times and in all places. There is a positive attribute to this kind of thinking; it is the assurance of the reality that is pictured in

---

2. Lindbeck, *Nature of Doctrine*.
3. Ibid., 17.

the statement. In other words, if the Bible contains a collection of true propositions, then they can be extracted from its pages and historical context and applied directly to the contemporary setting. There are also a few problems with this approach to reading the Bible: What is a reader to do with contradictory statements in the Bible itself? What is a reader to do with obvious statements that are not congruent with what is known as reality in the twenty-first century? How is the truthfulness of a proposition verified? What is a biblical reader to do with a propositional statement that is obviously not true (are parts of the Bible to be discarded)? And finally, why do people even believe that the Bible should be read as a book of propositions?

A few examples from the Bible will be used to explore how a propositional understanding might prove problematic. The first example comes from Matthew 5. In this chapter, Jesus addresses the topics of anger, adultery, divorce, oaths, retaliation, and love of enemies. All of these issues are addressed by first stating a proposition or biblical principle from the past and then giving a new imperative. Readers of these texts are left with the dilemma of what to do with the texts from the Hebrew Scriptures. If the Old Testament statements are straightforward propositions, then they are literal propositions in the first century with Jesus and his hearers. If Jesus is challenging these ancient statements, then were they ever an accurate picture of the way the moral universe operates? Does this mean that the Hebrew Scriptures are not on a par with the New Testament? Dilemmas such as this are what Marcion (d. ca. AD 160) attempted to overcome when he limited the Scriptures to a very small canon, but the church quickly considered him a heretic. A few other examples can also be given: What is a contemporary reader of the Scriptures to do with clear statements about women in leadership? Or slavery? Or how do the words and actions of Jesus correlate with the idea of violence in many parts of the Old Testament? And what is a reader to do with the cosmological statements in various parts of the Bible? Contemporary persons know that the sun does not revolve around the earth and that there is not a dome called sky that keeps the water above from overwhelming the earth.

These comments do not mean to imply that there are no propositional-like statements in the Bible; there are. Perhaps it might be better to recognize these statements as confessions of faith. It is the judgment of this author that the ancient communities of faith made these confessions based upon both the inspiring activity of God and the worldviews within which these communities of faith found themselves. This would allow for a development of these confessional statements and the ideas they contain in the unfolding of the story of God. A great example of this is found in Deuteronomy 6:4-5, the Shema: "Hear, O Israel: The Lord is our God, the Lord alone. You shall love the Lord your God with all your heart, and with all your soul, and with all your might." This imperative implies for its most ancient hearers that no god is to come before Yahweh in loyalty and devotion. This did not necessarily exclude the idea of other deities existing in the framework of reality, but none of these deities were to have any control or say in Israel's life. The Shema was Yahweh's exclusive claim upon Israel's life. In the unfolding of time, this mandate developed into a deep belief in the singularity of Yahweh as the only divine reality. Yahweh is not only exclusive in the devotion of the people but also singular in reality. This confession was then transformed to some degree by early Christians. As early as the first century, followers of Christ were worshipping Jesus, and by the early fourth century, orthodoxy confessed that God was triune: Father, Son, and

Holy Spirit. Although Christians understand the triune God as one, Jews who practice the confessional prayer of the Shema understand this oneness differently.

A reader of the Bible must investigate ways to incorporate the truthfulness of ancient confessions while also leaving room for the dynamism of the ways these confessions are handed down through time. All three of the confessional understandings associated with the Shema are true, and yet there is room for development. These expressions of the Shema build upon one another. One might say that there is within the confessions of the Bible a depth of grammar that is able to "go on" speaking in new settings with new worldviews.

George Lindbeck also describes a way of doing theology as experiential-expressive. What he means by this expression is that a theological statement is a linguistic expression of a prelinguistic experience, and in the case of the Bible, this experience is of God. This approach to doing theology comes from the father of modern theology and hermeneutics, Friedrich Schleiermacher. An example of this can be seen in an approach to reading the book of Jonah. The author of Jonah, according to the experiential-expressive scheme of interpretation, had an experience of God in which he came to believe that God was gracious, merciful, slow to anger, abounding in steadfast love, and ready to relent from punishing. He says as much in the concluding section of the book: "He prayed to the LORD and said, 'O LORD! Is not this what I said while I was still in my own country? That is why I fled to Tarshish at the beginning; for I knew that you are a gracious God and merciful, slow to anger, and abounding in steadfast love, and ready to relent from punishing'" (4:2).

When this methodological approach is used to read the Bible, an interpreter reads the words of the text in their ancient cultural setting and worldview with the goal of uncovering the universal religious experience of the author. This methodological procedure is described as demythologizing the ancient biblical text. This prelinguistic experience then is reimagined into a contemporary setting with all of the implications of the present-day culture and worldview. If revelation is acknowledged in this method, it is understood as a prelinguistic experience of the Divine. God communicates in nonlinguistic ways to the subjective experience of an individual. Two problems emerge from this method: First, how can a contemporary interpreter ever discover the nonlinguistic experience of an author? And second, how can persons even have an experience apart from the linguistic framework they participate in? This is not the approach that is recommended in this book.

George Lindbeck's third methodological approach is called cultural-linguistic. This methodology believes that a person's experience becomes meaningful based upon the language and therefore the culture that a person participates in. An example of this can be seen in the English words "ice" and "snow." An indigenous person who lives in the arctic will experience much greater detail in encountering ice and snow than will an indigenous person who lives in the tropics. The indigenous person who lives in the tropics will not have the linguistic categories to make sense of his or her encounter with ice and snow. Lindbeck is indebted to the linguistic turn in philosophy that took place in the latter half of the twentieth century. He is particularly dependent upon the thinking of Wittgenstein. This operational methodology recognizes experience as derivative of language rather than prior to language. Language is what conveys experience to consciousness. This does not mean that there are no sensations that take place in human beings, but that their meaning and perhaps even their recognition are language dependent. What this indicates is a move away from the subjectivity of the individual and a shift toward the linguistic community. Wittgenstein makes it clear that there is no private language: "But could we also imagine a language in which a person could write down or give vocal expression to his inner experiences—his feeling, moods, and the rest—for his private use?—Well, can't we do so in our ordinary language?—But that is not what I mean. The individual words of this language are to refer to what can only be known to the person speaking; to his immediate private sensations. So another person cannot understand the language."[4]

The absence of a private language concerning even sensations means that context is vital in the interpretation of Scripture. An interpreter must understand not only the events within which the texts emerge but also the culture and linguistic worldview within which the ancient confessions took place. Whatever phenomenon occurred, its meaning was made possible by the linguistic worldview of the people apprehending it. This implies that the actions of God in the world are interpreted by the linguistic frameworks available to people at that time. Worldviews are not detached from the larger form of life a people participate in but are enacted narratives with their own beliefs and value systems. They are linguistic dramas with their own sets of practices, symbols, stories, and exemplars. Readers of the Bible must place themselves imaginatively into the matrix of these ancient worldviews and make every effort to perceive the responses to the ancient words. This tethered imagination is essential to understanding the witness of Scripture.

---

4. Wittgenstein, *Philosophical Investigations*, sec. 243.

Understanding a pericope[5] Christianly must not only take place within its historical context but also within its larger canonical context. When a passage of Scripture is understood in the light of the whole Bible, which is fulfilled in Jesus the Messiah, its Christian meaning comes into focus. As the Christian meaning of an individual passage is construed in the light of the whole story of God, it becomes the linguistic framework to experience the world as God's world. This is what Paul Ricouer means by the second naïveté.[6] An individual's experience will be Christianly mediated by his or her participation in the embodied story of God or, as Lindbeck writes, "the ancient practice of absorbing the universe into the biblical world"[7] will have taken place.

Conclusion

This chapter has attempted to combine the historically long development of Scripture with the theological conviction of divine revelation. The chapter title is the assumption of combining these two concepts: God leads his children along! Revelation takes place in space and time with real people in concrete historical situations who have the linguistic lenses of ancient worldviews. Revelation is not magic, but it is God's grace—the grace to see and to hear the movement and sounds of God in the world. It comprises the gifts of eyes to see and ears to hear what others see and hear differently. Yet the eyes and the ears are human eyes and ears—eyes and ears that are conditioned by the times they participate in. Ancient words from an ancient world

---

5. A pericope is a set of verses that forms one coherent unit or thought from a text.

6. Paul Ricoeur, *Symbolism of Evil*, 351.

7. Lindbeck, *Nature of Doctrine*, 135.

bear witness to the One who is the Alpha and the Omega, the Beginning and the End!

THREE

What Does the Bible Want Us to Know?[1]

When present-day persons read the story of Abraham enacting a promise in the mysterious journey of his life, what is it in this Bible story that is relevant for today? When a person recites the Twenty-Third Psalm at the bedside of a sick friend, what is to be found in this strange poetry from long, long ago? When the stories of the resurrection appearances of Jesus are read on an Easter morning, what does the Bible long to proclaim?

> What is the significance of the remarkable line from Abraham to Christ? What of the chorus of prophets and apostles? And what is the burden of their song? What is the one truth that these voices evidently all desire to announce, each in its own tone, each in its own way? What lies between the strange statement, In the beginning God created the heavens and the earth, and the equally strange cry of longing, Even so, come, Lord Jesus![2]

Given the previous chapter, which articulates how narrative frameworks shape human understanding and mean-

---

1. This chapter was inspired by the ideas of the great Swiss theologian Karl Barth.

2. Karl Barth, *The Word of God and the Word of Man*, trans. Douglas Horton (Gloucester, MA: Peter Smith, 1978), 31-32.

ing, the question that a modern-day reader desires to ask is, What is in the Bible that is vital for the twenty-first century? This chapter will attempt to explore this question and a subsequent question that addresses the difference that reading the Bible has for understanding the world. In order to answer these questions, this chapter will inspect various features within the Bible to see if they are appropriate subjects to explore. The chapter will then discuss how the Bible itself yearns for its reader to read it and understand the world.

What Is in the Bible?

There are different reasons why people read the Bible. Some individuals feel a religious obligation to read the Scriptures. Reading the Bible functions for them as a religious or moral duty that endeavors to please God. Other persons read the Bible for inspiration and emotional well-being. For those who long for comfort and assurance, the poetry and promises of the Bible pull them like gravity toward confidence and hope. Others read the Bible for instruction on how to live pragmatically in the world. They believe that the Bible contains the wisdom of heaven on how to prosper on earth. Principles are extracted from the "Good Book" and applied, like a self-help manual, to one's life. Many people understand the Bible to be a moral textbook or guide. Again, principles are discovered and extracted from the pages of this ancient book and applied to one's moral activity. Others read the sacred texts for their historical relevance. Understanding the course of history is not only an awareness of the past but also a chart for the future. Still others read these texts in an attempt to discover the proper ways to worship the God of Abraham, Isaac, and Jacob and the God and Father of the Lord Jesus Christ. There are even people who attempt to read these ancient texts for scientific understanding. They attempt to discover facts that will contribute to a truthful cosmology. The church has often read and used these texts to excavate them for theological source material. There are all of these reasons and many more for reading the Bible, but how does the Bible want its reader to read it? To answer this question, three categories of inquiry will be explored: history, science, and morality.

There is no question that the Bible is a historical book; all language is historical. Words have their meaning only in the way they are used in a particular space and time; therefore, all words are understood in a historical setting. The reader of the Bible cannot understand the message of a prophet, storyteller, letter writer, or even a lawgiver without understanding its historical setting. In addition to this, the Bible narrates a history of a people: They are called to be a people in Abraham and were delivered from bondage out of Egypt. They conquered the land of promise, experienced exile and return, and gave birth to a first-century Jewish male who was considered by many to be the Messiah. His story is historical. He preached the kingdom of God, healed the sick, drove out demons, was involved in controversies, taught disciples, and was crucified. The Bible narrates the history of a people.

The Bible is a historical collection of writings, but what is a reader to do with the narratives that seem to describe the story with places and times that are contradictory to one another? An example of a different chronological order of events can be demonstrated by comparing the Synoptic Gospels' narration of the cleansing of the temple and with the Johannine Gospel's account of this event. The dissimilarities between the two narratives insinuate an obvious problem. While the Synoptic writers place the cleansing of the temple during the last days of Jesus's ministry, John positions it as early as the second chapter of his Gospel, or

The Bible clearly can only make sense in the framework of a certain space and a particular time. Words and concepts have meaning only in their use, and the use of a word is contextual.

at the beginning of Jesus's ministry. This earlier position-
ing would alert the reader to Jesus's critique of and conflict
with the religious system of first-century Judaism. It is very
unlikely that Jesus would have driven the traders out of
the temple on two different occasions, and thus the biblical reader is forced to ask which account gives the correct
historical timeline. The inquiry as to when the cleansing
took place is a justifiable question, but it may also cloud the
message of why John places the episode early in his Gospel.
Perhaps John understands this event as a declaration that
the temple is defiled and therefore unfit for the worship
of God. The Johannine Gospel is written late in the first
century, well after the fall of Jerusalem and the destruction
of the temple. What seems most important is the theological message of the sacred texts, which is clearly shaped by
historical context.

What does all of this mean for the reader of the Bible?
The Bible clearly can only make sense in the framework of
a certain space and a particular time. Words and concepts
have meaning only in their use, and the use of a word is
contextual. A reader of the Bible aspires to understand the
different contexts within which the words were used. What
was going on when these words were spoken? What was the
worldview that the words emerge from? What was the value
system that the words both confront and reflect? These
questions and many more are historical questions essential
to understanding the biblical text, but is history the reason
the Bible was written? Perhaps the purpose of the Bible has
to do with something much weightier than obtaining historical data of what might have transpired.

If the purpose of the Bible is not unearthing historical
details, then is it a book that attempts to make scientific
sense of the world? There is no question that the pages of
the sacred text deal with the topic of God's creative design

of reality. The very first words of the Bible state, "In the beginning when God created the heavens and the earth" (Gen. 1:1). God is acknowledged as the creator of all reality, but what is the purpose of this confession? Is it simply a scientific deposit of information about the beginning of the universe? There is no question that the biblical texts in Genesis, Proverbs, Job, many psalms, the Gospel of John, Colossians, and Hebrews point to the certainty that the God of Israel is the originator, designer, and purpose maker of the world. The One who liberated Israel from Egyptian bondage, gave them a land, and revealed his will in the Torah is none other than the creator of the universe. Why is the confession of these ancient Jews, that their God is the creator of reality, so important?

The ancient world had a number of narratives about the derivation of the world. What is significant about these stories is that they at least convey a set of values that instigated the very act of creation. These values are within the ancient belief system and form a way of experiencing the world. One of the foundational stories that intersected the people of ancient Israel is the *Enuma Elish*. This poetic narrative is a Mesopotamian myth of creation that narrates the struggle between order and chaos. The fundamental story occurs in assorted configurations. An early version of this story comes from the ancient Sumerian Empire, and a later version is the Babylonian creation story. What makes this convergence of ancient Israel with this narrative so important is twofold: Israel's beginnings in Abram (Abraham) and the Babylonian exile. The story of Abram (Abraham) in Genesis 11:31 declares that he came from Ur of the Chaldeans, which was a part of Mesopotamia. The worldview of this story was a part of what Abram (Abraham) left, as recorded in Genesis 12. What is also of great importance for the ancient Jews who produced the Bible is the Babylonian captivity, which takes place well over a millennium after the events that the story of Abram (Abraham) recounts. Israel's history intersects with the people and worldview of the *Enuma Elish*.

The *Enuma Elish* portrays the creation of the world, which was brought about by a battle between gods. Following this cosmic battle, the carcass of the goddess Tiamat was used for the purpose of creation. Marduk splits her in half, "like a dried fish," and places one part on high to become the heavens, with the other half to be the earth. Humanity was created out of the blood of Kingu, who was the companion and general of Tiamat. Marduk mixed Kingu's blood with earth and used the clay to mold the first human beings. Humanity was to serve the gods as slaves. What is fascinating about this myth is that it narrates that chaos is vanquished by violence. One could sloganize the values of this story by saying, "Might makes right."

Ancient Israel's belief and value system was very different from that of its neighbors. Israel's creation stories described this foundational process without conflict, violence, and death. According to Genesis 1 and 2, the creation of the earth was for the sake of life itself. In the priestly account, a biosphere was created through forms of separation: light from dark, water from water, land from water. These acts of creation were for the sake of an environment, a place where life could flourish. Violence was nonexistent in this "good" creation. Even the act of sustaining life through taking in nourishment was nonviolent, as Genesis 1:29-30 states: "God said, 'See, I have given you every plant yielding seed that is upon the face of all the earth, and every tree with seed in its fruit; you shall have them for food. And to every beast of the earth, and to every bird of the air, and to everything that creeps on the earth, everything that has the breath of life, I have given every green plant for food.' And it was so." The act of creation was without conflict, violence, and death. It was for the purpose of being fruitful and multiplying; it was for the purpose of life. God is clearly depicted as pro-life in every possible way.

The wisdom tradition is also shaped by a creation theology. This tradition is consumed with the proposal that there are two ways in life: the way of wisdom and the way of folly. The way of wisdom leads to life, and the way of folly leads to death. Proverbs 8:35-36 affirms this deep conviction:

> For whoever finds me finds life
>> and obtains favor from the LORD;
> but those who miss me injure themselves;
>> all who hate me love death.

Why do the sages of ancient Israel hold this view of life and death? The answer is because they trusted that the created order corresponded to Wisdom herself. In verses 22-31, Wisdom articulates these words as she describes her role in creation:

> The LORD created me at the beginning of his work,
>> the first of his acts of long ago.
> Ages ago I was set up,
>> at the first, before the beginning of the earth.
> When there were no depths I was brought forth,
>> when there were no springs abounding with water.
> Before the mountains had been shaped,
>> before the hills, I was brought forth—
> when he had not yet made earth and fields,
>> or the world's first bits of soil.
> When he established the heavens, I was there,
>> when he drew a circle on the face of the deep,
> when he made firm the skies above,
>> when he established the fountains of the deep,
> when he assigned to the sea its limit,

so that the waters might not transgress his command,
when he marked out the foundations of the earth,
then I was beside him, like a master worker;
and I was daily his delight,
rejoicing before him always,
rejoicing in his inhabited world
and delighting in the human race.

Wisdom was created first, and then everything else
was created in and through her. She was understood to
be the paradigm within which creation takes place. To go
against Wisdom is to go against the very design of reality,
the created order. Conflict, violence, and death take place
in the wisdom tradition because of a repudiation of the
created order (Wisdom), not in order to create an order
(*Enuma Elish*). The creation texts of the Old Testament are
at least an argument against other narrative worlds and
their value systems. Practices, beliefs, and values emanate
from these ancient stories. Ancient cultures' forms of life
are the embodiment of these stories. Israel's form of life was
different; it was covenantal, which celebrated and protected
life. Many readers of Scripture focus on and argue over the
cosmological content of the Scriptures, but is this the issue
that is most important for the Bible? It is a very significant
aspect of the Bible, but it is not the heart of what the Bible
longs for its readers to know.

The Bible constantly refers to a moral way of life. The
Law and the Prophets point to this reality. The first five
books of the Bible are called the Torah, which means the
"law." Law is a way of ordering communal life; it is communal morality. The Prophets pronounce judgment oracles
upon both Israel, the covenantal people, and upon the
nations. These judgment oracles are a verdict upon unrighteous and unjust people groups. They clearly imply a moral

way of life. The New Testament is also concerned with an ethical way of life. Ethical living is discernable not only in the teachings of Jesus but also in the controversies that besiege him. The leaders and teachers of Israel continually accused him of immorality and ungodliness, based upon their interpretation of Torah. It should be remembered that all controversy stories are concerned with conflicting understandings of moral and theological issues. Jesus interprets the biblical story in a way that calls his followers to a form of life that fulfills the Torah and the Prophets, even though a great many religious leaders of his day interpret his words and actions as breaking with the Torah. For example, he says the following in Matthew 5:17-20:

> Do not think that I have come to abolish the law or the prophets; I have come not to abolish but to fulfill. For truly I tell you, until heaven and earth pass away, not one letter, not one stroke of a letter, will pass from the law until all is accomplished. Therefore, whoever breaks one of the least of these commandments, and teaches others to do the same, will be called least in the kingdom of heaven; but whoever does them and teaches them will be called great in the kingdom of heaven. For I tell you, unless your righteousness exceeds that of the scribes and Pharisees, you will never enter the kingdom of heaven.

Jesus was always teaching and modeling a moral way of life. He will take the moral vision to a place where it seems never to have gone: to turning the other cheek, to unlimited forgiveness, and to even loving one's enemies.

The apostle Paul is also committed to an extraordinary ethical form of life, even though he seems to argue against the Torah itself. He writes about the Torah in Galatians 2:15-21:

We ourselves are Jews by birth and not Gentile sinners; yet we know that a person is justified not by the works of the law but through faith in Jesus Christ. And we have come to believe in Christ Jesus, so that we might be justified by faith in Christ, and not by doing the works of the law, because no one will be justified by the works of the law. But if, in our effort to be justified in Christ, we ourselves have been found to be sinners, is Christ then a servant of sin? Certainly not! But if I build up again the very things that I once tore down, then I demonstrate that I am a transgressor. For through the law I died to the law, so that I might live to God. I have been crucified with Christ; and it is no longer I who live, but it is Christ who lives in me. And the life I now live in the flesh I live by faith in the Son of God, who loved me and gave himself for me. I do not nullify the grace of God; for if justification comes through the law, then Christ died for nothing.

Yet Paul, with all of his talk of justification apart from the law, still calls on churches to live into an exalted moral form of life. In Galatians 5:16-26 he writes these words:

Live by the Spirit, I say, and do not gratify the desires of the flesh. For what the flesh desires is opposed to the Spirit, and what the Spirit desires is opposed to the flesh; for these are opposed to each other, to prevent you from doing what you want. But if you are led by the Spirit, you are not subject to the law. Now the works of the flesh are obvious: fornication, impurity, licentiousness, idolatry, sorcery, enmities, strife, jealousy, anger, quarrels, dissensions, factions, envy, drunkenness, carousing, and things like these. I am warning you, as I warned you before: those who do such things will not inherit the kingdom of God.

By contrast, the fruit of the Spirit is love, joy, peace, patience, kindness, generosity, faithfulness, gentleness, and self-control. There is no law against such things. And those who belong to Christ Jesus have crucified the flesh with its passions and desires. If we live by the Spirit, let us also be guided by the Spirit. Let us not become conceited, competing against one another, envying one another.

This passage clearly contains ethical imperatives given by the apostle to his churches. These ethical imperatives are a system of laws, a way of structuring a community's life together.

No one who reads the Bible can doubt that it includes an intensely ethical form of life, but is the purpose of the Bible simply a collection of ethical rules and commands to be obeyed? Are all commands in the Bible of equal value to twenty-first-century believers? If not, how is one to read the Bible with a second naïveté? Before looking at the answer to this question directly, several legal and ethical laws need to be explored as examples of the problems that arise in understanding the Bible as a moral codebook.

There is no doubt that the Bible deals with certain aspects of human behavior and social constructions that appear to be morally repugnant to twenty-first-century readers. For the sake of this chapter, two passages will be explored for their moral content: a passage about holy war and a passage about adultery. After exploring these passages, several brief summary comments will attempt to bring this section of the chapter to a close, and then an answer will be given to the question, What is in the Bible that is vital for the twenty-first century?

If the values informing Israel's creation texts indicate that God creates without violence and therefore God is pro-life, then what is a modern reader of Scripture to do with the idea of holy war? A casual reader of the Bible will soon find that war and violence play a part in the unfolding story of Israel and her God. The compelling passage of 1 Samuel 15:22-23 is in response to King Saul's failure to follow through on the act of devoting to the ban the Amalekites and their king. These verses call all readers to total obedience:

> Has the LORD as great delight in burnt offerings and
>> sacrifices,
>> as in obedience to the voice of the LORD?
> Surely, to obey is better than sacrifice,
>> and to heed than the fat of rams.
> For rebellion is no less a sin than divination,
>> and stubbornness is like iniquity and idolatry.
> Because you have rejected the word of the LORD,
>> he has also rejected you from being king.

The concept in this passage, in 1 Samuel 15:3, and in the warring episodes of many other passages of Scripture that is most troubling is transliterated *cherem* or *ḥērem*, and it means "to devote to the ban." The clearest description of why the ban is used as a concept in ancient Israel is found in Deuteronomy 7:1-6:

> When the LORD your God brings you into the land that you are about to enter and occupy, and he clears away many nations before you—the Hittites, the Girgashites, the Amorites, the Canaanites, the Perizzites, the Hivites, and the Jebusites, seven nations mightier and more numerous than you—and when the LORD your God gives them over to you and you defeat them, then you must *utterly destroy them*. Make no covenant with them and show them no mercy. Do not intermarry with them, giving your daughters to their sons or taking their daughters for your sons, for that would turn away your children from following me, to serve other gods. Then the anger of the LORD would be kin-

dled against you, and he would destroy you quickly. But this is how you must deal with them: break down their altars, smash their pillars, hew down their sacred poles, and burn their idols with fire. For you are a people holy to the LORD your God; the LORD your God has chosen you out of all the peoples on earth to be his people, his treasured possession. (Emphasis added)

Many persons and societies have used this concept to justify the use of violence on individuals and people groups that they perceive as a violent threat to them. Clearly this is not the rationale for the use of *cherem* in this passage. The utter destruction of the people groups named here is not to protect the people from the risk of violence, but to eliminate the peril of failing to adhere to and obey God by turning to follow other gods. Turning to follow other gods would mean the people would become shaped by the worldviews and forms of life of the foreign gods. These different forms of life would for all practical purposes make Israel a different people and not a "people holy to the LORD" (v. 6). The admonition to not intermarry and to "break down their altars, smash their pillars, hew down their sacred poles, and burn their idols with fire" (vv. 3, 5) implies that they really would not kill all of the people. It was the different cultures with their value systems that were a threat to the people of God.

When this text is understood in its larger canonical context, which finds its completion and fulfillment in Jesus, the twenty-first-century reader must understand the use of violence ultimately in the light of Jesus's life and words. Matthew 5:38-48 details a variety of sayings of Jesus on violence:

You have heard that it was said, "An eye for an eye and a tooth for a tooth." But I say to you, Do not resist an evildoer. But if anyone strikes you on the right cheek, turn the other also; and if anyone wants to sue you and take your coat, give your cloak as well; and if anyone forces you to go one mile, go also the second mile. Give to everyone who begs from you, and do not refuse anyone who wants to borrow from you.

You have heard that it was said, "You shall love your neighbor and hate your enemy." But I say to you, Love your enemies and pray for those who persecute you, so that you may be children of your Father in heaven; for he makes his sun rise on the evil and on the good, and sends rain on the righteous and on the unrighteous. For if you love those who love you, what reward do you have? Do not even the tax collectors do the same? And if you greet only your brothers and sisters, what more are you doing than others? Do not even the Gentiles do the same? Be perfect, therefore, as your heavenly Father is perfect.

It should be clear to even the casual reader that Jesus in these words, as well as the way he conducted his life, did not favor the use of violence. The Bible should not be used to justify violence. If the Christian community is going to participate in violence, then some other rationale must be used to warrant its use.

What does the Bible have to say about adultery and rape? Here are the words of Deuteronomy 22:22-29 on these matters:

If a man is caught lying with the wife of another man, both of them shall die, the man who lay with the woman as well as the woman. So you shall purge the evil from Israel.

If there is a young woman, a virgin already engaged to be married, and a man meets her in the town and lies with her, you shall bring both of them to the gate of that town and stone them to death, the young woman because she did not cry for help in the town and the man because he violated his neighbor's wife. So you shall purge the evil from your midst.

But if the man meets the engaged woman in the open country, and the man seizes her and lies with her, then only the man who lay with her shall die. You shall do nothing to the young woman; the young woman has not committed an offense punishable by death, because this case is like that of someone who attacks and murders a neighbor. Since he found her in the open country, the engaged woman may have cried for help, but there was no one to rescue her.

If a man meets a virgin who is not engaged, and seizes her and lies with her, and they are caught in the act, the man who lay with her shall give fifty shekels of silver to the young woman's father, and she shall become his wife. Because he violated her he shall not be permitted to divorce her as long as he lives.

All of these laws have the common theme of sexual intercourse outside of the boundary lines of the covenant of marriage. The first law is concerned with any man having sexual intercourse with another man's wife. Both the man and the married woman are to die. The second law covers the possibility of the rape of an engaged young woman within the borders of a town. Again, both the man and the woman are to be executed. The rational for their execution is that the man violated the marriage of another man; it is never mentioned that he desecrated the woman. What amazes a twenty-first-century reader is that the woman is culpable because she was supposed to cry out and didn't. This law presupposes that if she resisted and cried out, someone in the town would have heard her. The third law describes a situation that is exactly like the previous law with one exception: the rape takes place outside of the town. The presupposition is that the woman did resist and cry out, but because she was in open country, no one could hear her. The implication is that her husband, the engaged man, was desecrated, but the young woman was not culpable. Only the man who raped the young woman is executed. The final law portrays a situation where a young woman who is not engaged—and therefore with no husband to be desecrated—is raped by a man. If the man and woman are caught, then the rapist is required to pay her father and marry her. Because the rapist violated the young woman, he is not allowed to ever divorce her. This seems to be the only law that understands the young woman as a victim with legal rights.

A twenty-first-century reader of these texts does not have to do much exegetical work to realize three things. First, ancient Israel believed that sexuality had clear limits on who could be involved in this act that was laden with the potential for procreation. Second, the judgments that involved extreme violence are completely out of bounds for today's world. Finally, women were not particularly significant from the perspective that executed judgment. These laws predominantly protected the paternity of children born into a marriage, not the dignity of women.

What are contemporary persons to do with these types of texts? This question is valuable not only to interpreters of these strange moral laws concerning sexuality but also to interpreters of a host of other moral laws that are concerned with a number of other moral categories. To eliminate all laws that seem to challenge contemporary receptivity is to end up a heretic like Marcion.[3] Another answer to the ques-

---

3. Marcion was an important figure in early Christianity. His theology rejected the deity described in the Hebrew Scriptures and in distinction affirmed the Father of Christ as the true God. His ideas are named after him. He taught that the God of the Old Testament was the author of evil, oppressive, and a lesser and distinct entity from the God of the New Testament, who exhibited love and

tion of what to do with these strange texts is to read them Christianly—that is, to read them in the light of the entire canon, with special attention to the words and actions of Jesus.

The New Testament has much to say about this moral category. Jesus's ministry seems to involve characters who are at least considered morally unfit because of sexual defilement. This does not necessarily mean that Jesus did not believe in sexual boundaries. Matthew 5:27-30 records Jesus as saying,

> You have heard that it was said, "You shall not commit adultery." But I say to you that everyone who looks at a woman with lust has already committed adultery with her in his heart. If your right eye causes you to sin, tear it out and throw it away; it is better for you to lose one of your members than for your whole body to be thrown into hell. And if your right hand causes you to sin, cut it off and throw it away; it is better for you to lose one of your members than for your whole body to go into hell.

Referring to this passage, does it mean that a person is to mutilate himself if his sexual temptations and passions are too strong? Some in the history of reading this text have done just that. This is not the recommendation that is being proposed. What is also interesting about this text is that

---

forgiveness. Because of this Marcion rejected much of what is considered the Christian Bible today. This includes a complete rejection of the Old Testament. Marcion accepted only eleven books of the Bible, which included an abridged Gospel of Luke. In his adaptation, he removed all references to the Old Testament, the Jews, and the humanity of Christ. He also included ten of Paul's Epistles: Romans, 1 Corinthians, 2 Corinthians, Galatians, Ephesians, Philippians, Colossians, 1 Thessalonians, 2 Thessalonians, and Philemon. The early Christian Fathers, Tertullian and Irenaeus, combated the heresies of Marcion. He was excommunicated in AD 144 or his radical views. Marcion was the first person who sought to establish a Christian canon of Scripture.

The subject of the Bible is nothing less than God and his story told from the perspective of God's ancient people. This story was whispered, written, and enacted across well over a millennium.

Jesus is changing the calculus of value in human sexual relationships. The man is addressed as the one who is responsible for seeing the woman as a person with dignity and rights. He cannot even look upon her with lust, as an object for his own gratification, without committing an act of adultery. In this text, the woman is not designated as married or even as engaged, but simply as human. Jesus challenges his culture's understanding of the very worthiness of women. Women, not just men, are entitled to human nobility.

To summarize this chapter, the opening question needs to be revisited: What is in the Bible? Clearly a reader of Scripture can find an answer to almost any question asked of the Bible. The Bible is historical and ethical and has a cosmology. If questions are asked from these categories, then the Bible will give its answer to those questions. The Bible also contains some of the most beautiful and inspiring literature that the world has ever read. It has a variety of worship practices and even visions and prayers to inspire and warn its readers. But is any of this the reason why the Bible itself beckons its readers to study its old, old pages? Perhaps none of the above categories is the reason why the Bible yearns to be read.

What Does the Bible Desire to Reveal?

The subject of the Bible is nothing less than God and his story told from the perspective of God's ancient people. This story was whispered, written, and enacted across well over a millennium. Throughout this extension of time, God opened the eyes of his people to discern him in the course of history and in the fabric of creation. One might say that God, through the inspiration of God's Spirit, left traces of Godself in the created order and in the unfolding of history. Over time, these glimpses of the mystery of God in creation and history formed and reformed a narrative that was constantly developing until the fullness of time. Finally, God's story became manifest in the flesh and blood of a first-century Jew named Jesus.

The extensive narrative of God is recounted by the people of Israel, who see the unfolding of events as episodes in a grand story of rescue and restoration. Alternative voices are given to witness to God across this long development through time. In a way, one could say that this story of God is self-corrective by the different perspectives of its witnesses, as they write and become actors in his grand story. In other words, it takes the whole story narrated through the canon to fully interpret any single portion of the Bible. The ancient people of God understood that the world is not simply a place where this historical narrative is enacted but also the property of their God: the God of Abraham, Isaac, and Jacob. He created it and sustains it. He placed within his creation an order that not only reflects his will but also is shaped by his very character. This understanding of the cooperative relationship between the Creator and his creation is described in the wisdom tradition and even early Christianity. There is no doubt that this is truly a Jewish story, but it is not only the story of the Jewish people but the story of their God as well. He is in every episode, even when his name is not spoken. Their heroes are all dependent upon him. Even the book of Esther, which does not even mention God, implies his presence in the unfolding of history. The Bible is the story of God told from the point of view, which is a worldview, of a people who believed the Creator elected them to be his people, with the mission of bearing witness to him and bringing his blessing to all of creation. Wow, what a book!

FOUR

Interrogating the Text

A mystery novel is a joy to read when the reader is taken through a series of twists and turns in the plotline, or when a character who is understood one way is exposed as another. The surprise and sense of delight happens because the reader is able to connect the dots of persons and events within the novel. There is a narrated logic to why the characters or plot goes in a surprising yet meaningful way. But when the change of character or direction happens without any connection to what has transpired in the novel, a reader is left with a sense of disappointment. The novel is not well written, because there are not adequate clues that point the reader in the direction of discovery.

If a reader were to approach the Scriptures as a detective, what questions would he or she ask the ancient biblical texts? Most probably the reader would put forward questions such as these: What happened? Where did it take place? What are the parameters of the events? How did it take place? Who was involved? What are the clues? Why did it occur? And what difference does it make? These are the kinds of questions that biblical exegetes ask of a passage of Scripture. Both this chapter and the next will use biblical texts as examples of how these questions are posed to a pericope. The reason for this is to show how the categories of interpretation foster understanding when used synergistically. This chapter will examine primarily questions of a historical and literary nature. In the next chapter, questions of a theological and ethical character will be considered. The questions and categories of this chapter are as follows:

A. Contexts
   1. Historical
      a. Events
      b. Worldviews
   2. Literary
      a. Immediate
      b. The Entire Book
B. Structure
C. Genre
D. Words and Concepts
E. Intention of the Passage
   1. What Is Overcome?
   2. How Is It Overcome?
F. Summary of the Passage's Message

Contexts

Historical Context

When exegetes explore the various settings of a pericope, they begin with the passage's history. Many biblical texts have long histories that include the occurrence that gave birth to the first confessional interpretation of the event, the assorted moments within the process of the oral tradition that transmitted the confessional story, the occasion that prompted the written document of the story, the editorial process of collecting various materials into a larger literary unit, and the different ways the biblical material was understood and used by interpreters. A great example of someone who does this kind of exegetical work can be observed in Brevard Childs's commentaries on Exodus

(1974) and Isaiah (2001). Also, within each of the moments of the historical development of a passage of Scripture, there are at least two major categories that must be explored: various historical events and the narrative worldviews connected with the major participants of the events. It is important to remember that worldviews contain beliefs and values and that these beliefs and values have a major role in shaping the interpretation of events. In other words, what a community believes about reality and what it values will shape how it understands the happenings that take place in and to the community.

The book of Isaiah will be used as an example of the complex historical and literary contexts that challenge the interpreter. According to 6:1, Isaiah received his call "in the year that King Uzziah died," which took place in 742 BC. Many, if not most, Old Testament scholars believe that only portions of chapters 1–39 can be assigned to the eighth century. Almost certainly chapters 40–66 come from a much later time and are known as Second Isaiah. Many scholars have an additional division made between chapters 40–55 and chapters 56–66. These historical-literary distinctions are known as Second Isaiah and Third Isaiah. Second Isaiah comes from the exilic period, and Third Isaiah comes from the postexilic period.

If, as many scholars believe, oracles were spoken by the prophet and others and then orally transmitted by a group of disciples across an extended time, this would imply that the narratives about the prophet and the poems contained within the book itself came together through the process of remembering, writing down, collecting, and finally arranging the material. The final composition of the book most probably came together in the fifth century BC, well after the return from exile. Exactly how three time periods came together is not known to historians, but this historical development seems to indicate that the original disciples developed a school of thought that would shape the vision of later generations of prophets. This is one way of explaining the extreme differences in writing style and historical references. What is of interest to modern exegetes is that the messages of the book are not overly dissimilar in theological content, but they do differ in literary style and historical reference. This development does not need to alarm anyone who believes that the Scriptures are inspired by God; God's work of inspiration was ongoing through this Isaiahic school of thought.

What is very important for the modern reader of Isaiah is to hear its messages within their historical settings. For example, Isaiah 40:1-2 makes the most sense in the light of a people who are in Babylonian exile. Listen to these words of hope:

> Comfort, O comfort my people,
>> says your God.
> Speak tenderly to Jerusalem,
>> and cry to her
> that she has served her term,
>> that her penalty is paid,
> that she has received from the LORD's hand
>> double for all her sins.

Hope is proclaimed into the lamentations of the people! Israel's God brings comfort because sins have been accounted for by the Almighty. Israel has a future, even while she waits in Babylon.

It is also possible to listen to this text in a later time, perhaps in the postexilic period, when it would have been collected into its final form. This should be done with a full awareness of the original setting of the oracle, but with the ongoing message to the disappointed Israelites in postexilic times. Remember that the book was most probably brought together in the fifth century. The vision of restoration seemed incomplete to Israel under the Persian Empire.[1] Hear the words of the latter half of the oracle in verses 27-31:

> Why do you say, O Jacob,
>> and speak, O Israel,
> "My way is hidden from the LORD,
>> and my right is disregarded by my God"?
> Have you not known? Have you not heard?
> The LORD is the everlasting God,
>> the Creator of the ends of the earth.
> He does not faint or grow weary;
>> his understanding is unsearchable.
> He gives power to the faint,
>> and strengthens the powerless.
> Even youths will faint and be weary,
>> and the young will fall exhausted;
> but those who wait for the LORD shall renew their
>> strength,
>> they shall mount up with wings like eagles,
> they shall run and not be weary,
>> they shall walk and not faint.

Hearing the oracle in this historical setting allows Israel to remember that the Babylonians did not have the last word and neither do the Persians. Yahweh, the Creator, has the first and last word, and therefore there is hope. The One who called them, judged them, and delivered them will fulfill the promises made to them in exile. Even though there are various historical contexts, the message when understood in the light of those contexts brings newness to the present moment of the reader. Which historical context is

---

1. Empire ruling during the postexilic period, which began in 538 BC, when Cyrus, the Persian emperor, permitted the return of Jews to Jerusalem.

most appropriate for interpretation? Both, when done with tethered imagination.

It is also indispensable to recognize the worldviews that are in conflict within the historical contexts. An example of this can be observed in the prevailing questions of the sixth century: What happened? And why did it happen? The Babylonians and their primary god, Marduk, from the vantage point of the narrative belief system of Babylon, defeated Israel and its God, Yahweh. How was Israel to comprehend this horrific occurrence? As related in chapter 3, the *Enuma Elish*, the Babylonian creation narrative, describes Marduk as defeating the forces of chaos by battling Tiamat, the primal goddess of chaotic waters. This act of violence then becomes the foundation for the creation of the world and human beings. As observed earlier, the value system this narrative world sustains is that creation and the abeyance of chaos is possible because of an act of violence—that is, in this narrative world, "Might makes right." When the mighty Babylonians defeated and destroyed Jerusalem and the temple in 587, the natural question to arise in the ancient world was, Did Marduk defeat Yahweh? If so, then the value system associated with the god Marduk was the value system of creation. If Marduk did not defeat Yahweh, then why was Israel defeated and in exile?

Answering this question, in the light of the narrative worldview of Israel, was of utmost importance for the belief system of Israel. The people would explore their narrative world with its events, concepts, and values. Within the tradition of the book of Isaiah, the school of prophets would reimagine the message of the eighth-century prophet. The answer to this question is that it was Yahweh, not Marduk, who defeated Judah and destroyed the temple. This act was not defeat, but judgment! Listen to the words found in Isaiah 1:10-20:

Hear the word of the LORD,
>   you rulers of Sodom!
Listen to the teaching of our God,
>   you people of Gomorrah!
What to me is the multitude of your sacrifices?
>   says the LORD;
I have had enough of burnt offerings of rams
>   and the fat of fed beasts;
I do not delight in the blood of bulls,
>   or of lambs, or of goats.

When you come to appear before me,
>   who asked this from your hand?
>   Trample my courts no more;
bringing offerings is futile;
>   incense is an abomination to me.
New moon and sabbath and calling of convocation—
>   I cannot endure solemn assemblies with iniquity.
Your new moons and your appointed festivals
>   my soul hates;
they have become a burden to me,
>   I am weary of bearing them.
When you stretch out your hands,
>   I will hide my eyes from you;
even though you make many prayers,
>   I will not listen;
>   your hands are full of blood.
Wash yourselves; make yourselves clean;
>   remove the evil of your doings
>   from before my eyes;
cease to do evil,
>   learn to do good;
seek justice,
>   rescue the oppressed,

defend the orphan,
    plead for the widow.

Come now, let us argue it out,
    says the LORD:
though your sins are like scarlet,
    they shall be like snow;
though they are red like crimson,
    they shall become like wool.
If you are willing and obedient,
    you shall eat the good of the land;
but if you refuse and rebel,
    you shall be devoured by the sword;
    for the mouth of the LORD has spoken.

Only a return to the covenantal values and practices of social justice, the care for the marginalized, would allow Yahweh's own people to "eat the good of the land."

Literary Context

The narrative plotlines of the Pentateuch and the Gospels are obvious places to observe the importance of literary context. There are sequences of events that occur within the larger story that seem dependent upon one another. Obvious examples can be detected in the Abram (Abraham) story. Chapter 15 of Genesis, the great covenant promise reinstated by God to Abram (Abraham), is dependent upon the call narrative and promise of chapter 12. Chapter 15 also sets up the disappointing and ruthless actions of Sarai (Sarah) and Abram (Abraham) in chapter 16 with Hagar and, in the larger narrative development, the journey to the mountain to sacrifice Isaac in chapter 22. This is a story that is dependent upon the tension of a plot to carry its characters to the end of the story. What careful readers notice is that there are only pauses, never completions, in these biblical stories. The reason for pauses rather than completions is that the stories are not first and foremost about the human characters, but they are a part of the story of God working with and through these human beings. Israel and early Christians understood themselves to be taking part in a grand narrative, not a story of their own scripting.

The purpose of literary context becomes a little more difficult to discern in the prophetic and wisdom material. Much of this material was organized by later disciples and sages around a theme or issue. This statement does not mean the material lacks literary and even theological importance. What needs to be appreciated is that its placement in a document is accomplished by a redactor for a purpose. These redactors use multiple stories, sayings, or poems in an editorial manner to create a single document. Redactors, or editors, develop coherence and purpose in their work usually for the sake of a specific community. These unique communities face specific problems and issues, and the redactors are attempting to use the material available to them to address these concerns. The question to ask is, Why is this saying or poem in this place in the document? For those who believe in the work of the Spirit in the development of the Bible, this becomes one more opportunity to see the wisdom of God at work among his people. It must be remembered that the inspiration of Scripture is not a onetime event, but an ongoing activity of God's Spirit through the entire development of the Bible.

The book of Isaiah is a good example of how this understanding of redaction brings meaning to the text. The historical context of Isaiah 40 is during exile. It is a time of great lamentation for Israel, and it begins with these words:

Comfort, O comfort my people,
   says your God. (V. 1)

But what does the redactor of the book of Isaiah want the reader to notice? Chapter 39, which historically is located in the eighth century, ends with words from King Hezekiah: "Then Hezekiah said to Isaiah, 'The word of the LORD that you have spoken is good.' For he thought, 'There will be peace and security in my days'" (v. 8). Isaiah 39 describes an event that took place over hundred years prior to Israel's exile. This passage describes an incident where Babylonian envoys came to King Hezekiah because they heard he had been sick. The king welcomed them and showed them his treasure house and armory. It was in response to this that the eighth-century prophet spoke to the king these words as recorded in verses 5b-7: "Hear the word of the LORD of hosts: Days are coming when all that is in your house, and that which your ancestors have stored up until this day, shall be carried to Babylon; nothing shall be left, says the LORD. Some of your own sons who are born to you shall be taken away; they shall be eunuchs in the palace of the king of Babylon."

When the redactor gathered these various texts from the Isaiah collection and placed them into an intentional order, he was attempting to show how the actions of a previous generation profoundly influenced a future generation. King Hezekiah was, on the whole, a good king, but his actions would create a future tragedy for Israel. What the redactor was also doing in placing these texts together was to proclaim that humanity does not have the last word. Yahweh, the Creator, has the first and the last word. In fact, Isaiah 40:8 declares, "The word of our God will stand forever."

This example from Isaiah is but one demonstration of how literary context becomes very important for the reader of the Bible. Because it is so obvious that literary context is vital in reading narratives containing sayings and laws, examples are not required to illustrate this observation. But apprehending the literary contexts of the Epistles is absolutely necessary for a faithful reader of the Bible. Most of the letters of the New Testament are communications to ancient communities of faith. The historical circumstances are certainly important, but so also are the literary contexts. A helpful way to think about a New Testament letter is to see it as an extended argument or at least a collection of arguments to a community of faith about specific issues that the community is facing. An argument is built step by step by thoughtful writers. What goes before in an argument is a base upon which later statements can rest. What was said in the letter as well as what will be said advances the larger coherence of the argument.

An example of this can easily be detected in Romans, between chapters 3, 4, 5, and 6. In chapter 3, Paul is arguing that the righteousness of God, which was attested to "by the law and the prophets" (v. 21), was disclosed "through faith in Jesus Christ" (v. 22). Using Abraham as an example, Paul builds on this argument in chapter 4. He uses a familiar "then" or "therefore" to move his argument along to describe Abraham as realizing the promise of God through faith. He states in verse 22, "Therefore his faith 'was reckoned to him as righteousness.'" He then ties this argument of faith and righteousness to the belief that Jesus's followers have "in him who raised Jesus . . . from the dead" for their justification (vv. 24-25). Chapter 5 extends the argument with the familiar "therefore" to include the results of justification. Romans 5:12-21 seems almost like an excursus from the argument, but if it builds upon what has gone before, then it advances what Paul is attempting to communicate. These verses in chapter 5 articulate the differences between Adam and Christ. Adam is understood as the progenitor of humanity; therefore, he will be understood as the old humanity. Christ is understood as the progenitor of the new humanity; therefore, he will be the source of the new life brought about by his resurrection. Paul is arguing that justification by faith in

Jesus is nothing less than participation in the new humanity. Chapter 6 begins with the familiar "therefore" to move the argument along. Paul now wants to argue that believers in the resurrected Messiah do not go on living in sin, not because they are under law, but because they are the new humanity. He uses the common practice of baptism to warrant his claim of death to the old humanity and birth to the new humanity.

These chapters from Romans should clearly demonstrate how important literary context is in reading the Epistles. If, by the way, Paul is making a rational argument in these opening chapters of Romans, then the difficult chapters of 7 and 8 should cohere to his argument. Literary context is vitally important in a reader's understanding of a passage of Scripture.

Structure

What is meant by the structure of a passage? In this section we will answer this question and display the anatomy of a few passages as examples. This subdivision will also examine the importance of establishing the framework of a passage, but before proceeding, it is important to establish the limits of a passage.

One of the first questions that a reader of Scripture must ask is, Where does a pericope begin and where does it end? To understand the importance of this question, think about a book of short stories. If a reader begins reading in the middle of a short story and stops reading in the middle of another short story, what will be the meaning of the reading? The reader will have to connect the culmination of one story with the beginning of another. A conclusion will be understood as the start of a plotline, and the middle of another story will be considered the end of the plotted sequence. In other words, the reader will need to make up a meaning for the fragmented and incoherent collection of words.

There are several ways to discern the beginning and the end of a passage. Narratives are easiest to recognize, since they move from one sequence to another. A sequence in an account is a unit of thought. It should be remembered that often a collection of stories is gathered together by a redactor for the purpose of a larger story line. Both the smaller account and the larger collection have unique meanings for the reader of Scripture.

The most difficult biblical material to discern separate units of thought is the prophetic material. Many times the limits of a passage can be discerned by its thematic elements. Themes such as idolatry, justice, judgment, and hope are all topics that can be discerned in the development of a prophetic oracle. Other ways of discerning the opening and closing of an oracle can be detected by stylistic devices. For example, in the book of Amos the prophet begins many oracles with a reference to a word coming from Yahweh. The prophet also closes many of his poetic sermons with the phrase "says the Lord." These literary devices are signs to alert the reader of the beginning and ending of a poem, but much of the prophetic material lacks these rhetorical strategies. The same can be said for much of the wisdom material in the Old Testament and the apocalyptic material in both Testaments. This difficulty is one of the reasons why contemporary readers need to read the Bible with the help of the community of scholars. Such scholars have dedicated their lives to reading and helping others read these ancient texts. One should not forget that if a reader begins reading in the middle of one passage and stops in the middle of a second passage, the reader will inescapably supply his or her own meaning to the fragmented and incoherent collection of words.

What is meant by the structure or anatomy of a passage? The simplest way to explain it is as an outline. An outline is similar to a skeleton because it determines the shape of a unit of thought. A body is not simply a skeleton but also muscle, fat, skin, and so on. These pieces of the body, in turn, are connected to one another by the framework, or skeleton, in such a way as to create a whole body. Without the contours of the skeleton, the body would be unrecognizable and would not function. Likewise, words, concepts, and rhetorical devices are placed in a sequence to create an intentionality that is recognizable by a hearer or reader. Uptake—that is, understanding an utterance or a written piece—is the goal of a speech act. A couple of examples from the Scriptures will be used to describe how structure works and why it is important.

The first example comes from the opening of the book of Isaiah. Isaiah 1:10-17 is understood by a great host of Old Testament scholars as an oracle that was combined with verses 18-20 at a later date to form a larger prophetic sermon. This passage demonstrates the complex nature of the composition of the prophetic material. It is possible that the eighth-century prophet himself combined these two sections into one oracle to create this powerful prophecy. The obvious structure of the oracle is as follows:

A. Verses 10-17: The cultic worship of Judah is worthless in pleasing Yahweh.

   1. Cultic practices are of no value for Judah.

      a. Verse 10: Calling Israel and her rulers Sodom and Gomorrah.

      b. Verses 11-13*a*: Israel's sacrifices are worthless.

      c. Verses 13*b*-14: Keeping sacred time is burdensome to God.

      d. Verse 15: Prayer is of no consequence.

2. Verses 16-17: Wash yourselves, and learn to do good.

B. Verses 18-20.

1. Verse 18: He is arguing about cleansing, but using sarcasm for his argument.

2. Verses 19-20: Be obedient and live; be disobedient and die!

What this revelation discloses is that purity or cleansing does not come from cultic activities, but by conformity to the will of Yahweh through obedience to his covenantal desire for social justice. This passage will be used as an example again in this chapter to explore how words and concepts carry meaning from the beginning to the end of a passage.

Another example of structure is found in Mark 10:17-31. This is the story of the rich person who comes to Jesus asking, "What must I do to inherit eternal life?" This episode can be divided into three subsections: verses 17-22, 23-27, and 28-31. The structure could be outlined as follows:

A. Verses 17-22: Jesus and the rich man in conversation.

1. Verse 17: Jesus is confronted by the rich man asking for instruction.

2. Verses 18-19: Jesus gives the instruction asked for by the man.

3. Verse 20: The man responds to Jesus's instruction.

4. Verse 21: Jesus gives further instruction.

5. Verse 22: The man responds by walking away in grief.

B. Verses 23-27: Jesus and his disciples converse.

1. Verses 23-24: Jesus makes a statement about the kingdom of God and wealth, and the disciples respond.

2. Verses 25-27: The disciples ask, "Who can be saved?" Jesus responds that only God is able to save humanity.

C. Verses 28-31: Jesus describes the benefits and values of the kingdom of God.

1. Verse 28: Peter describes the disciples' exodus from all attachments.

2. Verses 29-31: Jesus describes the benefits and values of the kingdom of God.

What these verses reveal is that different social structures can keep a would-be follower of Jesus from the demanding path of discipleship in the kingdom of God. The way of Jesus Christ, the kingdom, is contrary to all social structures in this present age. The structure makes it evident that the encounter with the individual rich person is not an anomaly, but an illustration for those who would follow Jesus the Messiah.

Genre

Readers of the Bible find it extremely helpful to recognize the type of material, genre, they are reading. The word "genre" designates a particular set of characteristics that are socially agreed upon and developed over time. When people speak or write, they are using social conventions to communicate their thoughts to others. Speaking and writing are not the only ways that language and its conventions are used. In addition to spoken words and written words, genre is a useful concept for understanding art, architecture, music, and many other socially conveyed categories. The two major categories of genre in literature are prose and poetry, and within these are many subcategories. Socially agreed-upon conventions within a narrative worldview are very important, if not necessary, for readers of the Bible to recognize.

Within the Bible are several literary categories: narratives, poetry, epistles, proverbs, apocalyptic writings, laws,

Within the Bible are several literary categories: narratives, poetry, epistles, proverbs, apocalyptic writings, laws, prayers, miracle stories, visions, dreams, and so on. Each of these categories has subcategories.

prayers, miracle stories, visions, dreams, and so on. Each of these categories has subcategories. For instance, in the narrative classification there are historical narratives, sagas, parables, and more. Each of these genre classifications prepares the reader or hearer to understand the way language is being used by the author or speaker. For example, if a person begins a story with "Have you heard the one about . . . ," the genre that is anticipated is a joke. Hearers are supposed to respond to the story as a joke, not a news report. Another example of how language is used might begin with "Long, long ago and far, far way . . ." This language usage is from some sort of saga or epic. A third example of how a story might begin in a way that is recognizable is "Today in England, the parliament . . ." In this case, the genre is probably a news report. None of these opening lines guarantee that the statements are true or false; they are merely ways to classify things according to their linguistic types rather than their specific contents.

The oral and written story of Jesus's death was of great importance to early Christians. The Gospel of Mark is the earliest of the biblical Gospels, and its narration of the passion of Jesus is much more extensive than any other episode in its story of Jesus. Although there is no unanimity about the scale of the pre-Markan passion story, 1 Corinthians 11:23-26 unmistakably makes it clear that the death of Christ was understood early on as extremely important:

> For I received from the Lord what I also handed on to you, that the Lord Jesus on the night when he was betrayed took a loaf of bread, and when he had given thanks, he broke it and said, "This is my body that is for you. Do this in remembrance of me." In the same way he took the cup also, after supper, saying, "This cup is the new covenant in my blood. Do this, as often as you drink it, in remembrance of me." For as often as

you eat this bread and drink the cup, you proclaim the
Lord's death until he comes.

Paul's use of the oral tradition, in which he was a participant, points to the importance of the passion of Christ.

The passion story, in all of the Gospels, attempts to
narrate a sequence of events that take place in the last hours
of Jesus's earthly life. What is interesting is how much
narrative space is given to the passion itself within all of
the Gospels. This amount of narrative space points to the
significance of the crucifixion for the early followers of
Jesus. A key question for readers of the Gospels is, Why was
Jesus executed? In answering this question, New Testament
readers are also asking, What is the purpose of his death?
Are these stories some sort of atonement theory? If so, then
how are readers to respond to this atonement? Is the passion designed to describe human culpability in the death
of Jesus? If so, then how are readers set up to understand
human beings, especially themselves? Is this long section
of the Gospels designed to expose the politics of Jerusalem
and Rome? If so, then are there ways to resist the political
pressure of these institutions within the first century? The
passion of Christ is undoubtedly narrating a sequence of
events that led to the death of Jesus, but it also has a purpose for its story. This purpose is possibly located in a genre
function. Rather than give quick answers to the questions
concerning the meaning of the crucifixion, readers need to
explore possible genre functions of this narrative category.

The parables of Jesus, another genre, have a different
function than the passion narratives. Parables convey a
truth about the nature of reality without narrating a sequence of observable historical events. For example, Luke
15 contains three parables describing the exuberance of
finding that which has been lost: the lost sheep, the lost
coin, and the lost son. Each of these stories is directing the

attention of the reader to celebrate the recovery of a lost item. The implication is that God celebrates the reclamation of lost persons and so should the people of God. This is the truth of the parables in Luke 15. Anything other than this truth is at best secondary to this primary truth. The readers of the parables are left at the end of the final parable with an unstated question: Will you celebrate the return of the prodigal? The parable narrates the father going out to the elder brother, who refuses to come into the house to celebrate the return of his brother. The parable then states, "Then the father said to him, 'Son, you are always with me, and all that is mine is yours. But we had to celebrate and rejoice, because this brother of yours was dead and has come to life; he was lost and has been found'" (vv. 31-32). There is a response that is implied in the singular truth of the story. Parables narrate a truth and solicit a response.

There are different types of oracles in the Prophets, the major genre categories are judgment oracles and salvation oracles. Both of these literary types of oracles are obvious in the prophetic material. Instead of focusing on these two wide-ranging genres, the next example will look at how some oracles are used in ironic ways. Amos 4:4-5 is an oracle that uses a call to worship from cultic functionaries to the pilgrims who journey to the cultic sites. Notice the mockery and cynicism in the oracle:

Come to Bethel—and transgress;
to Gilgal—and multiply transgression;
bring your sacrifices every morning,
your tithes every three days;
bring a thank offering of leavened bread,
and proclaim freewill offerings, publish them;
for so you love to do, O people of Israel!
says the Lord God.

If readers of the Scriptures fail to recognize the irony in the oracle in Amos, they will abandon any possibility of comprehending how it was understood by an eighth-century Israelite. If readers of the Scriptures neglect the purpose of the parables in Luke, they will fail to be grasped by their function. To misunderstand the purpose of a particular type of literature is to misappropriate the text. Genres are formed and reformed in the matrix of every story-formed world. A passage of Scripture cannot be properly comprehended apart from understanding these social conventions.

Words and Concepts

Readers of the Bible cannot understand the meaning of a passage of Scripture without understanding how words and concepts are used within the passage. This means that readers cannot simply go to a dictionary of their mother tongue and discover how a word is used in an ancient text written in a different language. Confusion consistently occurs when readers believe that a translated word means for the first recipients what it means for them. Many challenges exist for twenty-first-century readers of the Bible. These challenges include the following:

1. The Bible was written in two major languages, Hebrew and Greek, with some portions of it written in a third, Aramaic.

2. The Bible was written within the framework of various narrative worldviews, and most, if not all, of these worldviews are different from the worldviews of the early twenty-first century.

3. The Bible was developed through an extremely long process of expansion by a number of different people and traditions, and words and concepts derive their meanings from how they are used.

Before exploring how words and concepts are used in a biblical passage, it is important to understand that the Bibles used by modern readers were produced by scholars who worked carefully to determine the most reliable text of each passage. A specialized discipline that engages in the discovery of the best possible original Greek or Hebrew text is called textual criticism. For the New Testament alone, there are thousands of Greek manuscripts and many other fragments of these New Testament texts from which the current Greek New Testament is established. There are also thousands of ancient translations (Latin, Coptic, Syriac, and others) of many of these texts. All of these ancient texts were written by hand and were copied from earlier hand-written documents. It should be remembered that there was no printing press until the middle of the fifteenth century; therefore, there are textual differences between many of these numerous manuscripts. With all of these various writings and the multiple variations within them, how is a reader to determine the original texts of the Bible? Thankfully this work has been and is being done by uniquely trained scholars. For the average layperson, pastor, and even scholar, the findings of textual critics have become consistent and reliable. Although this book is not designed to instruct readers in the task of doing textual criticism, it does seek to make readers aware of this vital work—a work upon which most readers of the Bible rely.

A major challenge for the readers of Scripture is in determining the original meaning of a word or concept. As was stated earlier, the original languages of Hebrew, Greek, and Aramaic make the task of discerning the meaning of a word or concept more difficult for those who do not read these ancient languages. Most people read a translation of the original languages in their mother tongue. A further problem is that all translations have an element of interpretation within them. Even the mental translation of a scholar who knows the language is caught in the trap of interpreting for himself or herself the meaning of a word. What is a reader to do? Every reader, even a scholar, depends upon previous readers to begin to understand these strange words and concepts from a different language and worldview. Translating is the attempt, usually by a team of biblical scholars, to make clear the understanding of how a word is used by a particular biblical author. What untrained readers should never do is rely solely on one translation and on one or two biblical commentators. This reliance on a narrow range of resources happens usually because the translation and commentators have some point of familiarity and agreement with the beliefs, values, and opinions of the inexperienced reader.

The earnest reader of the Bible, who is not educated in reading the original languages, is advised to read from multiple translations. Usually it is advisable to read from a more or less word-for-word translation (such as the *New American Standard Bible* [NASB]) and from a more or less dynamic translation (such as the *New International Version* [NIV] or the *New Revised Standard Version* [NRSV]), which attempts to communicate the meaning of a sentence. After reading a passage of Scripture, the interpreter of the Bible will find it helpful to consult a biblical commentary. Commentaries help readers in several ways, not the least of which is to help readers understand how a word is used in a passage. Like translators of the Bible, commentators are also shaped by their own interpretive lenses or perspectives. No language user is able to see the world from God's point of view; everyone is conditioned by the matrix of the narrative linguistic world that he or she lives within. This does not mean that a reader should not use the work of others, but it does mean that a reader should use the scholarship of a variety of others.

Along with using commentaries, a reader of the Scriptures needs to use a biblical concordance. There are many online, easy-to-use concordances that not only allow the reader to see how a word is used in different places within the Scriptures but also connect the reader to the original languages of the Bible. A person should always attempt to see how the word in the ancient languages of the Bible is used. If, for example, Paul uses a particular Greek word in a sentence, then the reader of this Pauline text needs to see how this Greek word is used in several Pauline passages. It is important to see how the word in the original language is used, not its translated counterpart. A reader of the Scriptures should first focus on how the word is used in the particular book of the Bible being studied. Then it is valuable to see how the word is used in other biblical books by the same author. If the reader understands the particular tradition the material participates in, then it is useful to see how a particular word is used in the tradition as a whole. Finally, it may be helpful to see how other biblical writings use the word. Often, words are understood and used differently by different authors and traditions within the Bible.

An example of how to explore the meaning of words and concepts in a passage will be presented using Isaiah 1:10-20. This pericope has an interesting collection of words and concepts for the exegete to consider. Verse 10 has two different couplings of words: (1) "rulers" and "people" and (2) "Sodom" and "Gomorrah." What is important about the use of these two cities is that they are used as a metaphor. They have been destroyed by the judgment of God for more than a millennium by the time the prophet speaks to Judah. Isaiah, in the eighth century, is pronouncing judgment upon Judah for similar reasons that Sodom and Gomorrah were judged. Verse 11 is addressing the concept of worship through the sacrificial system with the use of words such as "sacrifices," "burnt offerings," "fat of fed beasts," and "blood of bulls." This verse is also addressing the concept of Yahweh being unresponsive to these sacrifices with phrases such as "what to me is . . . ," "I have had enough . . . ," and "I do not delight in . . ." Verses 12-14 continue the concept of cultic worship practices by moving to the categories of sacred space and time. The concept of sacred space is communicated in these phrases: "When you come to appear before me . . ." and "Trample my courts no more." The idea of sacred time is expressed in words such as "New moon and sabbath and calling of convocation" and "Your new moons and your appointed festivals." There is also a return to the idea of sacrifices as seen in the phrases "bringing offerings is futile; incense is an abomination to me." A major clue to what is going on in this passage is introduced in verse 13 with the term translated "iniquity." This word is one of the major expressions for sin in the Old Testament. It denotes systemic or structural malevolent practices that produce an immoral ethos within a culture. A person is understood as iniquitous because he or she is infected with this immoral societal ethos. When the people participate in the cult practices at their worship centers and yet participate in iniquity, they are judged by Yahweh. Their worship is meaningless.

Verse 15 brings the concept of prayer into play with the phrases "When you stretch out your hands . . ." and "even though you make many prayers. . ." Yahweh's response to these prayers is "I will hide my eyes" and "I will not listen." The reason is given in a twofold artistic expression: "your hands are full of blood." This phrase implies not only the blood associated with the sacrificial system but also, most importantly, the blood associated with social injustice. The concept of social injustice will be stated in a more ostensive way in the next two verses of the oracle. Verses 16 and 17 make apparent the iniquity of Judah in various phrases and words. The alleged sin of the people of God is first expressed as "remove the evil of your doings." It is then stated as "cease to do evil, learn to do good." What should be apparent to the reader is that doing evil and doing good are two forms of life that are in conflict with one another. To not do the good is to participate in doing evil. This can be seen in the social practice expressed in the next phrases: "seek justice, rescue the oppressed, defend the orphan, plead for the widow." The social structure that the prophet is demanding, in the name of Yahweh, is one that actively protects and cares for the vulnerable and powerless in society. Vulnerability is a concept expressed in words such as "oppressed," "orphan," and "widow." This is a seek-ing of justice. "Wash yourselves; make yourselves clean" (v. 16) is the concept of removing the iniquity that defiles the sociopolitical structure of eighth-century Jerusalem.

If this description of words and concepts is correct, then the metaphors of "Sodom" and "Gomorrah" will correlate with the concept of social justice, which is caring for vulnerable people. Turn to Genesis 18 and 19 and notice what both Abraham and Lot do with the messengers who come into their social contexts; they bring these sojourn-ers into their homes with hospitality and protection. Also notice the use of the covenantal terms "righteousness" and "justice." These terms are used in relation to the vulnerable. An often-used phrase in the Hebrew Scriptures refers to caring for the widow, orphan, and stranger. This is exactly what Abraham and Lot were doing and what the men in the city failed to do; therefore, judgment came upon Sodom.

Isaiah 1:18-20 forms a section that likely was added to the oracle at a later date. This does not mean that it lacks integrity with the notion of the oracle; it corresponds to the rest of the poem as an intense thought-provoking conclusion. The words and concepts that are so important to this section include the color red, as seen in the words "scarlet" and "crimson." This color concept denotes a twofold idea: blood, therefore violence, and a stain that is difficult, if not impossible, to remove. A second concept is purity or whiteness, as can be seen in the words "snow" and "wool." The phrase "let us argue it out" indicates in this poem the process of thinking through the probability of something happening. Is it probable that stained material can become pure again? The rhetorical function of this section is not a promise that it can, but a sarcastic remark that it cannot! This sarcasm can be seen in the next collection of words and concepts. The phrase "willing and obedient" is to be understood in juxtaposition with "refuse and rebel." In other words, if the community does what is right in relation to justice and righteousness, then it will live, "eat the good of the land." The opposite is also true; if it fails to live within the covenant policies of Yahweh, then the people will be "devoured by the sword." This is not about individual behavior, but the social structure and behavior of the community as a whole. These last two verses make it obvious that obedience to the covenantal ways of Yahweh is necessary for the survival of the people of God. Judah misunderstood the function of worship, believing that through the practice of worship, God could be placated and ultimately manipulated.

Clearly, understanding Isaiah's use of words and concepts and how they are used in the anatomy of the oracle itself is necessary in determining the sense of the passage.

Intention of the Passage

What is meant by the intention of a passage of Scripture? In a postmodern world where many literary critics believe that the reader is sovereign over the text, the ques-

A contemporary reader must remember that these words, concepts, and rhetorical strategies were understandable to persons who heard them in the ancient world. A word cannot mean today what it could not mean when it was uttered or written.

tion emerges, Can a contemporary reader know the mind of an author? An honest answer is, probably not. Then what can twenty-first-century readers recognize within a passage of Scripture that can be described as the intention of the pericope? A contemporary reader can know a few things about a biblical text. First, and foremost, an actual text is being read. This text is a part of a canon; therefore, it is concrete and unmovable. Contemporary persons are not the authors of the church's sacred texts, but the readers. There is a book in the church, and it is called the Bible. Second, a biblical passage of Scripture has historical and literary contexts to be explored. These contexts often point to the sociopolitical issues of the ancient world, but they also indicate the worldviews informing the ancient texts. Third, a contemporary reader can discern the genre of a passage of Scripture and the ancient function within its linguistic matrix. Contemporary persons can know that proverbs are proverbs and not laws, that apocalyptic is apocalyptic and not history, and that epistles are letters and not sagas. Different categories of literary material have diverse functions! A present-day reader can know, to some degree, the social conventions working through the language of a passage of Scripture. Finally, one can become acquainted with the way words, concepts, and rhetorical devices were used by a particular author or tradition. A contemporary reader must remember that these words, concepts, and rhetorical strategies were understandable to persons who heard them in the ancient world. A word cannot mean today what it could not mean when it was uttered or written. All of this exegetical effort is not for its own sake, but for the purpose of developing a "tethered imagination" to recognize the intention of a biblical passage of Scripture. A tethered imagination is not meant to stifle the creativity of a reader, but to anchor the reader's imagination historically so that he or she can envision an ancient world and reenvision his or her own in the light of it. Two questions that may be helpful in this imaginative work are, (1) What is overcome in the text? And (2) how is it overcome?

What Is Overcome?

To ask what in a text is overcome is to recognize the dilemma or issue the text is addressing. People communicate for a reason, and hearers interpret words based upon their understanding of the motivation of an utterance. For example, if a speaker says "You're on fire," there is an intending toward something. If the speaker is a nurse who has just taken a patient's temperature, but the patient interprets the statement to mean fire is consuming her body, then there is probably a problem with uptake[2] in the communication process. If a firefighter says to a person in a burning building the same thing, and the person interprets the utterance to mean she is attractive, there is a major problem in communication. Some issue or dilemma is governing the intention of the communication. To not understand the concrete situation is to misunderstand the speech act. Therefore, the reader's response to what is said or written will be different from what is intended.

Confusion is also very probable when there is misapprehension of the type of language game being used. For example, when a college student says to his date when he picks her up "You're on fire," what does he mean? If he is using this expression as a metaphor to communicate that she is very attractive, but she interprets the expression as sarcasm to mock her new hat, there is a serious communication breakdown. This misinterpretation can lead to very different responses to the utterance being used. The same

---

2. See p. 108.

confusion applies when reading a parable and interpreting it as if it is a historical narrative or when reading a proverb and interpreting it as if it is a prophetic oracle or even a law. This does not mean that all of these genres are not intending toward something that is truthful, but that these various literary types are communicating a "truth" very differently.

So how does a reader understand the intention of a biblical passage by means of contexts, genre, and words and concepts? In order to describe this activity, an example from Isaiah 5:1-7 will be used. This oracle is a poetic parable. As a parable, its function is to draw the hearer into the poetic narrative and shift the point of view of the listener. Here is what this song of the vineyard declares:

Let me sing for my beloved
    my love-song concerning his vineyard:
My beloved had a vineyard
    on a very fertile hill.
He dug it and cleared it of stones,
    and planted it with choice vines;
he built a watchtower in the midst of it,
    and hewed out a wine vat in it;
he expected it to yield grapes,
    but it yielded wild grapes.

And now, inhabitants of Jerusalem
    and people of Judah,
judge between me
    and my vineyard.
What more was there to do for my vineyard
    that I have not done in it?
When I expected it to yield grapes,
    why did it yield wild grapes?

And now I will tell you

what I will do to my vineyard.
I will remove its hedge,
      and it shall be devoured;
I will break down its wall,
      and it shall be trampled down.
I will make it a waste;
      it shall not be pruned or hoed,
      and it shall be overgrown with briers and thorns;
I will also command the clouds
      that they rain no rain upon it.

For the vineyard of the LORD of hosts
      is the house of Israel,
and the people of Judah
      are his pleasant planting;
he expected justice,
      but saw bloodshed;
righteousness,
      but heard a cry!

The context of this oracle is twofold: historical and literary. The historical context emerges out of eighth-century Judah and addresses the social configuration of the culture that has allowed for abuse of the weak and marginalized. The literary context will reaffirm the unjust arrangements of power and resources in Judah. The next few verses, which make up a new oracle, reaffirm this issue of broken social arrangements:

Ah, you who join house to house,
      who add field to field,
until there is room for no one but you,
      and you are left to live alone
      in the midst of the land!
The LORD of hosts has sworn in my hearing:
Surely many houses shall be desolate,

large and beautiful houses, without inhabitant.
For ten acres of vineyard shall yield but one bath,
and a homer of seed shall yield a mere ephah.
(Vv. 8-10)

These two contexts make it clear that social injustice is a key concern in Judah.

These are the key words and concepts of this poem:

1. "My beloved" and "my love-song" (v. 1).
2. Vineyard.
3. "Choice vines," "a watchtower," "a wine vat" (v. 2).
4. "He expected it to yield grapes, but it yielded wild grapes" (v. 2).
5. "What more was there to do for my vineyard?" (v. 4).
6. "I will remove its hedge. . . . I will break down its wall. . . . I will make it a waste. . . . I will also command the clouds that they rain no rain upon it" (vv. 5-6).
7. "And it shall be devoured. . . . and it shall be trampled down. . . . it shall be overgrown with briers and thorns" (vv. 5-6).
8. "For the vineyard of the LORD of hosts is the house of Israel, and the people of Judah are his pleasant planting" (v. 7).
9. "He expected justice, but saw bloodshed; righteousness, but heard a cry!" (v. 7).

Clearly this parable is an extended metaphor and the words used are all pointing to the uselessness of a cared-for vineyard that produces undesirable grapes. This language becomes concrete toward the end of the poem when it names Israel and Judah as the loved and cared-for vineyard of Yahweh. But he expects it to produce the fruit of justice and righteousness. The social arrangements that do not produce justice and righteousness are judged and condemned. The key for the reader of this oracle is to ask, What was expected of the people as a whole? What did they fail to do? This should be discovered in the book of Isaiah itself, especially in the first thirty-nine chapters of the book. The majority of these chapters belong to the eighth century. What is overcome in this oracle? Social injustice is the problem to be overcome, and perhaps what must be overcome first is the lack of awareness that the hearers have of the injustice in their social arrangements. This oracle would most probably address persons and structures within the community that acquire resources at the expense of the marginalized and poor.

How Is It Overcome?

The second question that needs to be answered about the intention of the text is, How is the issue overcome? In this passage (Isa. 5:1-7) the problem of injustice, whether known or unknown, is overcome with a reference to the future act of Yahweh. God will judge the community for its excessive unfair ways, whether it knows they are unjust or not. A judgement oracle is designed to describe the action of God in righting a group of people. This text implies that God will remove his providential protection from the community and allow the forces of history and nature to take over; Judah will be devoured! The point of the parable is that justice is anticipated and that judgment is built within the very prospect of that expectation. Before any hermeneutical application can take place between the text and the context of the contemporary reader, an understanding must develop about the intention of a biblical passage.

Summary of the Passage's Message

After interrogating a biblical passage, it is valuable for a reader to write out in his or her own words the succinct message of the pericope. Ultimately, what a summary of a passage of Scripture is attempting to accomplish is to locate the pericope in the larger narrative world of the ancient faith community. The opportunity to address the passage's significance for the twenty-first century will take place following a clear understanding of the text's ancient message in its historical context.

Isaiah 5:1-7 will be used once again to demonstrate how a particular aspect of exegesis is accomplished. This passage is a parable-poem preached by the eighth-century prophet to confront Judah during a time of immense intimidation by the Assyrian Empire. Additional threats also befell Judah by other smaller kingdoms as a result of the empire's oppressive tactics. The response of Judah to this form of intimidation was twofold: hasten to the temple of Yahweh with offerings and piety to win his favor and/or make alliances with other small kingdoms. Both of these reactions were to ward off the terrorizing tactics of Assyria and other smaller nations. The prophet, as the herald of Yahweh, rejects both of these reactions. Yahweh's word, through the mouth of Isaiah, is that the threat to Judah is not Assyria or her neighbors' kingdoms, but her unjust social fabric. Judah failed to do righteousness and practice justice. The metaphor of a vineyard, which refers to Judah and Israel, is used to draw the hearers of Jerusalem into the covenantal value system that is the backdrop of the prophet's ministry. In the parable, vineyards have a purpose—to produce sweet grapes. But if the grapes are wild, then the vineyard does not function according to its purpose. It is of no use to the winegrower; its hedges and walls will be removed. Protecting the vineyard is no longer necessary.

The prophet then redescribes the parable: the vineyard is Israel and Judah, and the fruit of this vineyard is to be justice and righteousness. Judah does not need to intensify its worship or make alliances with its neighbors, but it must produce in its political and covenantal makeup justice and righteousness. In the larger literary context of eighth-century Isaiah, justice and righteousness will be described in economic categories that eliminate greed and extend fairness and generosity in the very ways the community constitutes its sociopolitical life under the covenant. The poor and marginalized are prioritized by the eighth-century prophets. The implication of the parable is that Yahweh will protect and care for his justice-producing vineyard called Judah. If his people do not practice justice and righteousness, then the protection, as depicted in the images of hedges and walls, will be removed.

Clearly, the message of a biblical passage is contextual in space and time. An ancient message is for a specific people concerning a precise issue within which they are entangled. But one might ask, What about the enduring message of a passage of Scripture? Does the parable of the vineyard have significance for a contemporary reader? If it does, then how is a reader of the Bible to make the jump from the eighth century BC to the twenty-first century AD? What must be remembered is that the meaning of a passage cannot signify what it could never have suggested to the ancient community of faith. So how is one to overhear the ancient message as God's word for today? These are the questions that will occupy the thoughts of the next chapter.

Overhearing the Text

FIVE

If the Bible is a collection of sacred writings that speak to issues in particular historical situations, then is it possible to hear the voice of God through these ancient texts today? An honest reader of the Bible acknowledges that there is not one passage of Scripture written with the twenty-first century in mind. Yet Jewish and Christian adherents read these ancient words with the expectation that they are going to be addressed by none other than God! What does this expectation mean? How is this possible? Is there an enduring message? Or is the message whatever a reader deems it to be? The purpose of this chapter is to explore the relevance of the Bible and its message for contemporary persons and to ask, How is one to *overhear* the ancient message as God's word for today?

To answer the above questions, this chapter is divided into two major sections and a short theological conclusion. The first section will explore the theological content of the biblical texts themselves. This is not initially an investigation into what a text means today, but what the text most likely meant in its ancient settings. In the second section, a Christian hermeneutic—that is, a Christian approach to interpretation—will be proposed to allow for the text's theological grammar to address the contemporary community of faith. The goal is to overhear the ancient message with contemporary Christian ears. For both of these sec-

The Bible directs the reader to ask a most important question: How does a particular passage of Scripture witness to the self-disclosure of God?

tions, passages of Scripture will be used to describe how a reader may go about exploring and answering these critical questions. The conclusion to this chapter will make a theological faith claim about the work of God in Christian hermeneutics.

The Theological Content of the Biblical Text

What is the theology of a passage of Scripture? The premise of this question is that all of the biblical passages made theological sense to their earliest hearers and readers. Therefore, the inquiry is concerned with the belief system of the ancient community of memory in the light of its own narrative framework and historical situation. This ancient perception included a vision of how God works in creation and history and how the community is to respond to God's activity. To explore the theology of a biblical passage, three questions are suggested for the biblical reader to ask:

1. How does the passage describe God?
2. What is the need or issue the passage is addressing?
3. How does the passage shape the ancient community's response to God?

This section will describe each of these questions and portray its use in several passages of Scripture.

How Does the Passage Describe God?

From the beginning of this book, the argument being made is that divine revelation is the self-disclosure of God in creation (space) and history (time). The Bible is the linguistic witness of ancient communities of faith—Israel and the early followers of Jesus—to this self-disclosure. This permanent record of these witnesses, the Bible, directs the reader to ask a most important question: How does a particular passage of Scripture witness to the self-disclosure of God? There are many passages of Scripture where the answer to this question is self-evident, but there are other passages that need a more nuanced description.

The self-evident answer can be observed in texts such as John 3:16-17: "For God so loved the world that he gave his only Son, so that everyone who believes in him may not perish but may have eternal life. Indeed, God did not send the Son into the world to condemn the world, but in order that the world might be saved through him." This text clearly witnesses to the self-disclosure of God in the person of Jesus the Messiah. The passage states plainly that God loves the world, God gives his Son, God does not condemn the world, and God desires to save the world. This description is made in view of the passage's larger context, which is the story of Jesus's encounter with Nicodemus. The story states that the saving activity of God is understood through such concepts as "the kingdom of God" in verse 3, "being born from above" in verses 4-7, and "the Spirit" in verses 5-8. When these words and concepts are brought into view, the passage indicates that the love of God for creation donates the Son, who establishes the kingdom to reverse the destruction of death and the devastation of that which condemns. God is revealed through Jesus as the lover and restorer of the world!

Another verse that seems apparent in its context is Matthew 5:48: "Be perfect, therefore, as your heavenly Father is perfect." The question that the biblical reader is called to ask and understand is, What does "perfect" mean in this context? If the interpreter of the passage understands the perfection of God to be God's impassibility or immutability, then the reader will believe that the injunction implies that he or she is summoned to a life free from suffering and change. But, in the larger context of chapter 5, if the reader understands the perfection of God to be God's love for creation that extends even to enemies, then perfection takes on a very different connotation. Perhaps the loving of enemies has conceptually built within it the potential for suffering, a suffering love that goes all the way to the cross. The passage witnesses, in Jesus, to God's perfection, which loves even enemies!

Philippians 2:4-11 is a passage that is a little more difficult to understand as it concerns the image of God. Is the conceptual image of God described in this Christ hymn understood in the self-emptying of Jesus or in the exalting activity of God, who is finally described as the Father?

Let each of you look not to your own interests, but to the interests of others. Let the same mind be in you that was in Christ Jesus,

> who, though he was in the form of God,
>> did not regard equality with God
>> as something to be exploited,
> but emptied himself,
>> taking the form of a slave,
>> being born in human likeness.
> And being found in human form,
>> he humbled himself
>> and became obedient to the point of death—
>> even death on a cross.

> Therefore God also highly exalted him
>> and gave him the name
>> that is above every name,
> so that at the name of Jesus
>> every knee should bend,
>> in heaven and on earth and under the earth,
> and every tongue should confess
>> that Jesus Christ is Lord,
>> to the glory of God the Father.

Is God disclosed in the self-emptying activity of the incarnation and in the obedience of the Incarnate One that would take him to a cross? Or is God revealed in the exalting activity associated with the resurrection? The answer to this question is the key to understanding the self-disclosure of God in creation and history. It seems that the answer to the above questions is yes to both! God is disclosed in the life, death, and resurrection of Jesus the Messiah.

Another passage of Scripture that is unique in witnessing to the self-disclosure of God is the book of Jonah. Literarily this text narrates the resistance of a prophet to proclaim a judgment oracle. This story also includes a thanksgiving poem in chapter 2 and remnants of a communal confession of faith in 4:2. The prophet is commanded to go to the city of Nineveh, the capital of Assyria, and "to prophesy against it." The interesting twist in the book is that the prophet attempts to flee from the presence of God by going "in the opposite direction" from the great city of Nineveh. While fleeing from the presence of God, a colossal tempest ensues and the sailors, recognizing that it is no conventional storm, discover "that Jonah is to blame." The prophet concedes "this and states that if he is thrown overboard, the storm will cease." The sailors refuse to do this and continue rowing, but all their efforts fail, and they eventually throw Jonah overboard. As a result, the storm calms, and the sailors then offer sacrifices to God.[1]

"Jonah is miraculously saved by being swallowed by a large fish," in whose belly he spends three days and three nights. While in the great fish, "Jonah prays to God in his affliction and commits to thanksgiving and to paying what he has vowed. God then commands the fish to vomit Jonah

---

1. Story of Jonah quoted or paraphrased from Karen A. Atkins, *The Book of Daniel and Jonah* (Bloomington, IN: Xlibris, 2010), 74.

out." God again commands Jonah to travel to Nineveh and "prophesy to its inhabitants. This time he goes and enters the city," proclaiming, "Forty days more, and Nineveh shall be overthrown!" (3:4, NRSV). After Jonah preaches this judgment oracle across Nineveh, "the people of Nineveh believe" and repent and clothe themselves in sackcloth. Their king does the same and sits in ashes. These are signs and symbols of repentance and mourning. God becomes aware of their repentance "and spares the city. Displeased by this, Jonah refers to his earlier flight to Tarshish while asserting that, since God is merciful, it was inevitable that God would turn from the threatened calamities" that he manipulated Jonah to preach. The prophet "then leaves the city and makes himself a shelter, waiting to see whether or not the city will be destroyed. God causes a plant . . . to grow over Jonah's shelter to give him . . . shade from the sun. Later, God causes a worm to bite the plant's root" and it shrivels. "Jonah, now being exposed to the full force of the sun, becomes faint" and pleads for God to kill him.[2] God then says, as recorded in 4:9-11,

> "Is it right for you to be angry about the bush?" And he said, "Yes, angry enough to die." Then the LORD said, "You are concerned about the bush, for which you did not labor and which you did not grow; it came into being in a night and perished in a night. And should I not be concerned about Nineveh, that great city, in which there are more than a hundred and twenty thousand persons who do not know their right hand from their left, and also many animals?"

How does this story describe God? God is described as one ready to bring justice on the unjust city of Nineveh, using various aspects of creation (a storm, sailors, a fish, a

---

2. Ibid.

plant, a worm, the inhabitants of Nineveh, and Jonah himself) to accomplish his goals and purposes; as one willing and able to change his mind; and as the one who causes things to grow or makes them great: waves, fish, cities, and even plants. The use of "to make great or grow" is used by the book of Jonah as a wordplay from the Hebrew word *gādal* (4:10). Conceptually, God, in the book of Jonah, is depicted not only as sovereign over creation and history but also as one who works through secondary causes to accomplish his will.

What is of special interest to the reader of Jonah is that God is envisioned as changing his mind about the city. He liberates Nineveh from what seems to be his intention of destroying the city. This change is not because of some arbitrary decision that God makes, but it is based upon the unchanging character of God as the prophet confesses in 4:2: "He prayed to the LORD and said, 'O LORD! Is not this what I said while I was still in my own country? That is why I fled to Tarshish at the beginning; for I knew that you are a gracious God and merciful, slow to anger, and abounding in steadfast love, and ready to relent from punishing.'"

There are other passages of Scripture in which Christianly interpreting God's self-disclosure is much more difficult. A distressing example of this is found in 1 Samuel 15, the rejection of Saul by God as King over Israel. Verse 3 states, "Now go, attack the Amalekites and totally destroy all that belongs to them. Do not spare them; put to death men and women, children and infants, cattle and sheep, camels and donkeys" (NIV). Saul only partially destroys the Amalekites, and because of this, he and his descendants have lost God's favor to rule over Israel.

Wow, how is a Christian reader of Scripture to interpret this passage? Clearly, in this passage, the character of God demands that Israel devote to the ban (Hebrew, *che-*

rem) the Amalekites and their king. What does this mean for a Christian understanding of God? Does this passage give permission to Christians to use violence? Does God use violence toward adversaries? How does a Christian balance this picture of God with the character of Jesus and his words and actions of nonviolence? Does the moral character of God change from the Old Testament to the New? Is the Incarnate One a different God from the God who created the universe and called and liberated Israel? These questions will be addressed in the second section of this chapter, but it should be noted that the character of God seems to diverge not only in this passage but also in several passages of Scripture.

What Is the Need or Issue the Passage Is Addressing?

After exploring the description of God in a biblical passage, a faithful reader will benefit greatly by asking, What situation(s) and/or issue(s) prompted the speaking or writing of a particular pericope? Passages of Scripture arise and are transmitted out of the midst of historical circumstances. These historical circumstances are extremely important in a reader's attempt to comprehend the message(s) of a passage of Scripture. The challenge for a reader is at least threefold:

1. When is an interpreter to date a particular passage in the Bible? Is it when the story, oracle, or saying first occurred? Is it during the process of oral transmission? Is it when the event occurred that brought about the first written expression of the passage? Or is it even when the events happened that occasioned the written expression of the Scripture in its final form? *All of these* are legitimate moments in history to explore the meaning and ongoing inspirational activity of the Spirit of God in the transmission of the text. A question that might be

helpful in thinking through the theological intention of the biblical text is, Does the picture of God depicted in the passage change if the text is read in a new context? Perhaps the most consistent reading of these texts will occur when the various historical contexts paint a very similar picture of God's character and activity.

2. A second challenge is found in the question, What is the human issue that the historical circumstance prompts? For example, is the issue fear, greed, prejudice, unfaithfulness, doubt, intolerance, injustice, or hopelessness? This question is most appropriately asked in one of the historical contexts of the text's transmission. It is also helpful to examine how the picture of God interfaces with this issue. What is God doing in relationship to this human dilemma? Is God forgiving, judging, liberating, comforting, or promising? This will illuminate the theological witness of the biblical text. A key question to ask is, Does the human problem change in the different historical contexts of the transmission of the passage of Scripture? If it does, then these issues become open subjects to be explored by the faithful readers of the Bible. If the issue remains the same in different contexts of transmission, then the reader can feel confident that the human problem is one to be investigated in the light of the self-disclosure of God witnessed to in the passage of Scripture.

3. A third challenge is to ask, What are the voices and concerns left out of a passage of Scripture, and why? What is meant by this is not an arbitrary transporting to the text the concerns of the twenty-first-century reader, but given the historical contexts and worldviews, who are the unnoticed

people? Why are their voices and concerns overlooked? Does the worldview of the ancient text conceal their affliction? For example, when a passage of Scripture addresses males, why are female concerns disregarded in the text? Are the interests of women simply ignored in an ancient male-dominant world? If the world is no longer dominated by male bias, what does the text say to those unheeded interests of women?

Another example is the issue of slavery. When a slave owner is addressed, as in the book of Philemon, how is the welfare of the slave Onesimus understood? Is this short letter advocating for slavery? Or do Onesimus-like people have fundamental value beyond simply the economic benefit for their owners? Further theological reflection will be needed in texts like this when twenty-first-century Christians read and yet understand the immorality of misogyny, slavery, violence, and other such issues.

A final example concerns the issue of righteous and unrighteous individuals and groups. This issue might be understood within the following question: Do unrighteous persons have concerns or issues that can be addressed even if such persons are not addressed directly in the text? Is there anything that unrighteous persons can hear that brings a sense of worth and value to their lives?

A great example of this can be discerned in Luke 15, the story of the waiting father. Unmistakably the passage is addressing the issue of discrimination by righteous Jewish people of those who have by circumstances or even by their own choices been excluded from the gathered people of God. Verses 1-2 states, "Now all the tax collectors and sinners were coming near to listen to him.

And the Pharisees and the scribes were grumbling and saying, 'This fellow welcomes sinners and eats with them.'" The story directly speaks to those who exclude others, but it indirectly speaks to those who find themselves defiled and excluded by their actions and place in Jewish society. What are their issues, and how does the self-disclosure of God address such people in the context of their unrighteousness?

In this parable, the obvious answer is that God searches for the lost and rejoices when they are found. What this implies is that God cherishes the lost in a way that is demonstrated even in their lostness. The value of unrighteous and defiled persons begins, not when they turn from their misguided and evil ways, but in the character of God.

Many more examples could be given of those omitted or only indirectly referenced by the language of the biblical passage, but for a reader, it is important to remember to explore the issues of those who are not given a voice in the language and context(s) of the passage of Scripture.

How Does the Passage Shape the Ancient Community's Response to God?

Passages of Scripture not only arise out of human need and bear witness to the activity of God in space and time but also call a reader to respond. What exactly does a response to Scripture mean? Is the reader called to respond to the need or issue addressed within the passage, or is the reader called to respond to God? The answer to this question is that the reader is called to respond to God.

The impediment in this understanding of a response to God and not to a human need is most obvious in the section of Scripture known as the Law. Undoubtedly obedience is the apparent response to law, but perhaps obedience is a subsequent response to grace. Deuteronomy 5:6 is the opening verse of the Decalogue and provides the ancient community of faith the reasoning for its obedience: "I am the LORD your God, who brought you out of the land of Egypt, out of the house of slavery." What is the motivation of Torah? Gratitude! It is God who has made the Israelites his people, and therefore they are called to respond to their liberation from slavery as graced people. Obedience is ultimately not an act that makes human beings God's people but a response to God as his people.

Earlier in this chapter John 3 was used as an example of how the character of God is portrayed. Clearly the issue or need the passage is addressing is a perishing and condemned world. God is depicted as one who loves, gives, and saves through the Son and his establishment of the kingdom. This passage is calling for the reader to respond, not to the need by overcoming a perishing and condemned world, but to God, who is overcoming a perishing and condemned world, by believing. This is clearly not a call to believe in belief or even a generic belief in the existence of God, but to believe that God is acting in Jesus to overcome the disaster of death and condemnation. Believing is actively trusting in the work of God in Christ, and this active trust is expressed in a form of life. One can look and see what a person believes and trusts.

Another passage of Scripture that was explored earlier is the book of Jonah. What is the response that this prophetic book is calling its readers to make? Is it to *believe* that God is going to enact justice upon an unjust world? Clearly this is a part of the Jonah story, but not the ultimate response the book calls its readers to make. The readers of Jonah already believed that God is the judge who makes the world right. One only has to casually read the Prophets to hear this again and again. Was the response *to go* where God called people to go and not attempt to sail to parts unknown? The ancient reader already knew that God calls his people to go to parts unknown—to places God would show them (see Abraham's story). Was it to *confess* that God was gracious, "merciful, slow to anger, and abounding in steadfast love, and ready to relent from punishing" (4:2)? These words quoted from Jonah are a confession of faith that Israel already knew about God's character toward it. So, what is the response that the book of Jonah wants from its readers? It is to *recognize and accept* that the character of God's grace and mercy extends even to the most awful people groups in the world. God loves Nineveh and relents even from destroying the great capital of Assyria.

How does this acknowledgment work itself out among God's people? Is it simply head knowledge, or does this type of knowing entail something more? Perhaps as a community of faith, which is called to reflect the character of God, Israel is to put flesh and blood on God's profound care for the dreadful, horrific, and appalling of this world. Possibly Jesus's call to love the enemy in Matthew 5 is not a new thought about God and human beings who are to be like God, but a restatement that ancient readers of Jonah already knew. It seems a proper response to the text to participate in God's love for all of creation, even the deplorables!

A final example comes from Isaiah 11:1-9 with its future expectations. The expectation of this poem is that God will raise a leader who will vanquish violence. The result of this is *shalom* for all of creation: "The wolf shall live with the lamb" (v. 6). A key question is, How do futuristic texts want the reader to respond? Are readers given a mystery puzzle to solve? Or are readers simply told that everything will work out in the end? God will take care of the future, so don't worry.

Perhaps there is a picture of tomorrow so powerful that the past (all that has been) no longer controls the choices that a person or community can make? Possibly the picture of God's tomorrow beckons believers into the mystery of the hidden nature of God and the hope that God will accomplish his purpose for creation. Faith and hope in God's future purpose could very well summon people into an active participation with God, who is remaking the world. Eschatological hope draws its readers into a future like a flame draws a moth or a magnet draws metal. The future, not the past, becomes the determining factor for choices made in the present. The questions to ask are, What is God doing? And how can God's people participate?

A Christian Hermeneutic

This chapter division will look at the earlier three questions, but through a contemporary lens. First, the description of God in the passage will be examined in the light of two explorations: What does the entirety of the Bible say in relation to this passage's picture of God? And how does the manifestation of Jesus Christ bring fullness to this conceptual picture of God? The second of the three questions, which has to do with the need or issue the passage is addressing, will be explored in the light of contemporary issues or needs that correspond to the ancient issues or needs. The ancient world and the contemporary world are very different, but perhaps they share a family resemblance in relation to concerns and needs. The third and final question will consider how the message is to be appropriated. Special care will be given to emphasize that the response is to God and his activity and not to the hardship or privation that the passage or contemporary setting describes.

Describing God Christianly

The great majority of passages in the Bible describe God in comparable ways. For example, the Scriptures are consistent in their witness to God as the creator of the heavens and the earth. God is also understood as the protagonist of the story of Israel and early Christianity. God is bringing creation to its intended purpose. Also, Jesus is not identified by his early followers as an afterthought in Israel's narrative history, but as its fulfillment. Therefore, the Hebrew Scriptures are not superseded by the New Testament but form the identity narrative within which the Second Testament is its scriptural conclusion. The Old Testament and the New Testament are not two stories, but a singular story about the Creator, who is bringing to completion his purpose and will for creation in the establishment of the kingdom in the person of Jesus.

The problem of interpretation occurs when specific witnesses within the Bible seem to contradict one another. An obvious example is the elucidation of violence in the Bible. God appears to advocate violence in the concept of holy war in the Old Testament; yet God seems to be unequivocal in his disdain for violence in the teaching and life of Jesus. For example, when Jesus says "Love your enemies" in Matthew 5:44, he at least means don't kill them. Other contradictions are not as obvious as this category of violence, but they are still refutations. A couple of examples of these rebuttals are (1) the differences between Proverbs and Job in the wisdom tradition and (2) the conflicts over resident aliens in the books of Ezra and Nehemiah, on the one hand, and the very different perspective in the books of Malachi, Ruth, and Jonah, on the other hand. What is a reader to do with these undeniable incongruities?

If one reads the Bible as a plenary narrative of God's revealing activity in Israel and Jesus, then it is the whole of

Scripture that must interpret the parts of Scripture. The problem is that one cannot read the whole of Scripture without reading its parts; yet to comprehend the parts, a reader must grasp in some fashion the whole. It takes most persons more than a lifetime to comprehend the sacred texts. Therefore, contemporary readers of the Bible recognize that these sacred texts must be read with the community of saints and scholars of past generations. What this involves is a lifetime of reading and praying the Scriptures with the *communio sanctorum* (Latin, "communion of saints").

A few instances will be given in order to explore this canonical reading. First, Proverbs and Job are literary expressions of the wisdom tradition in ancient Israel. Proverbs, which represents stock wisdom, expresses an understanding of cause and effect in relation to living a righteous or an unrighteous life. A general summary of this causal understanding goes something like this: When a person or community walks in the way of wisdom, blessing and life are the results. But when one walks in the way of folly, curse and death are the results. The problem arises, not when this is seen as a truth, but when it is absolutized as a universal truth claim. The argument then is that a person or community experiencing a deathlike state of affairs has walked in the ways of folly and unrighteousness.

Job becomes a corrective for reading Proverbs in this propositional manner. The book of Job is not communicating that folly does not lead to death, but that deathlike states of affairs are not all the result of folly. The "friends of Job" are defending stock wisdom in their dialogues in the book of Job, but the reader of Job knows that Job has not walked in the ways of folly. Job is a righteous man who is being tested to see if he or possibly anyone would serve God if there is no reward for serving him. This does not negate the truthfulness of Proverbs when understood holistically, but a reader cannot absolutize the causal understanding of stock wisdom and extrapolate that to mean that anyone suffering has done something foolish or evil. When Proverbs and Job are read synergistically, a profound wisdom is conveyed.

What is a reader to do with the extremely troubling contradiction between sanctioned violence in the Old Testament and the nonviolence of the person and teaching of Jesus? Are parts of the Old Testament wrong? Has the Old Testament been eclipsed by the New Testament? These questions are reminders of the Marcionite heresy in the early church. Marcion believed that Jesus was the Savior of the world, and his interpretation of this salvation was shaped by his reading of the apostle Paul. Because of this understanding, he not only reconceptualized God as witnessed to in the Old Testament but also eliminated the Old Testament from the Scriptures, along with other parts of the New Testament.[3] This is not acceptable to anyone who believes in the plenary inspiration of the Bible, but the question for Christian readers still is, How is the sanctioned violence to be understood in relation to the life and words of Jesus?

A troublesome example of a text (briefly discussed in chap. 3) that needs Christian clarification is Deuteronomy 7:1-6:

> When the LORD your God brings you into the land that you are about to enter and occupy, and he clears away many nations before you—the Hittites, the Girgashites, the Amorites, the Canaanites, the Perizzites, the Hivites, and the Jebusites, seven nations mightier and more numerous than you—and when the LORD your God gives them over to you and you defeat them, then you must utterly destroy them. Make no covenant with them and

---

3. For more on Marcion, see chap. 3, n. 3.

show them no mercy. Do not intermarry with them, giving your daughters to their sons or taking their daughters for your sons, for that would turn away your children from following me, to serve other gods. Then the anger of the Lord would be kindled against you, and he would destroy you quickly. But this is how you must deal with them: break down their altars, smash their pillars, hew down their sacred poles, and burn their idols with fire. For you are a people holy to the Lord your God; the Lord your God has chosen you out of all the peoples on earth to be his people, his treasured possession.

What is a Christian reader to do with this text in the light of the words of Jesus in Matthew 5:38-48?

You have heard that it was said, "An eye for an eye and a tooth for a tooth." But I say to you, Do not resist an evildoer. But if anyone strikes you on the right cheek, turn the other also; and if anyone wants to sue you and take your coat, give your cloak as well; and if anyone forces you to go one mile, go also the second mile. Give to everyone who begs from you, and do not refuse anyone who wants to borrow from you.

You have heard that it was said, "You shall love your neighbor and hate your enemy." But I say to you, Love your enemies and pray for those who persecute you, so that you may be children of your Father in heaven; for he makes his sun rise on the evil and on the good, and sends rain on the righteous and on the unrighteous. For if you love those who love you, what reward do you have? Do not even the tax collectors do the same? And if you greet only your brothers and sisters, what more are you doing than others? Do not even the Gentiles do the same? Be perfect, therefore, as your heavenly Father is perfect.

The exclusive narrative world of the kingdom of God, fulfilled in Jesus Christ, demands an exodus from every other story-formed world that holds people captive.

How is one to read Deuteronomy 7 Christianly? This question has at least two replies for its answer: first, the threat or issue that is implicit in the passage itself needs description, and second, the text must be read in the light of the person of Jesus being its fulfillment (Matt. 5:17-20). What is the threat or issue being addressed in Deuteronomy 7? Is it how to conquer one's enemies? Perhaps the slaughter of children and infants is a sacrifice to God? Christian sensibility quickly replies no to both of these pseudo answers. The issue is addressed in the text itself: "for that would turn away your children from following me, to serve other gods" (v. 4). This is made even clearer when the passage states, "Do not intermarry with them, giving your daughters to their sons or taking their daughters for your sons" (v. 3). If the people are completely annihilated, then how would it be possible to intermarry? The implication is that a false belief system, with its practices and values, is the actual threat to the ancient people of God. If God's people are influenced by an alternative religious narrative, then that story will become their story and they will become a different people.

When this understanding of Deuteronomy 7 is read in the light of the fulfillment of the story of God in the person of Jesus, then the issue is still the same, but the means is radically different. Jesus calls would-be disciples to deny themselves, take up their cross, and follow him. This is still an exclusive claim Jesus Christ has upon his followers. Paul will make the same argument in relation to baptism in Romans 6 and in his confession in Galatians 2:19*b*-20: "I have been crucified with Christ; and it is no longer I who live, but it is Christ who lives in me. And the life I now live in the flesh I live by faith in the Son of God, who loved me and gave himself for me." There are different expressions of this realization that God's people are to abandon absolutely the former and alternative narratives and forms of life that they inhabited. The exclusive narrative world of the kingdom of God, fulfilled in Jesus Christ, demands an exodus from every other story-formed world that holds people captive.

If Jesus is the "wisdom of God" (1 Cor. 1:24), the "image of the invisible God" (Col. 1:15), then God's character is revealed in the first-century person of Jesus. This is the "rule of faith," *regula fidei*, which will ultimately lead the church to confess that God is Father, Son, and Holy Spirit. God reveals Godself by means of Godself. First John 4:1-6 states,

> Beloved, do not believe every spirit, but test the spirits to see whether they are from God; for many false prophets have gone out into the world. By this you know the Spirit of God: every spirit that confesses that Jesus Christ has come in the flesh is from God, and every spirit that does not confess Jesus is not from God. And this is the spirit of the antichrist, of which you have heard that it is coming; and now it is already in the world. Little children, you are from God, and have conquered them; for the one who is in you is greater than the one who is in the world. They are from the world; therefore what they say is from the world, and the world listens to them. We are from God. Whoever knows God listens to us, and whoever is not from God does not listen to us. From this we know the spirit of truth and the spirit of error.

The Johannine community was cautioned to test the spirits, so also the Christian reader of the Bible must discern the character of God in the Bible. This does not mean the Old Testament or even the New is to be interpreted in an allegorical manner, as if every passage discloses Jesus, but every passage is to be understood as fulfilled in Jesus Christ. He is the inauguration of the completion of the story of God. God is disclosed in Jesus: "And the Word became flesh and lived among us, and we have seen his glory, the glory as of a father's only son, full of grace and truth" (John 1:14). The person of Jesus, as narrated in the Gospels, is the plumb line for a Christian's understanding of God's character. When the Bible is read Christianly, a reader realizes that God's moral nature is disclosed in Jesus.

Hearing Humanity's Cry

Are human beings the same yesterday, today, and forever? In many ways a historian would say no. Ancient persons experienced the world in a different way than twenty-first-century persons do. They held different beliefs about the world and its place in the universe; they also were shaped by value systems that are in many cases repulsive to many, if not most, contemporary persons. Yet there is a family resemblance between ancient and present-day persons. People, both ancient and modern, feel dread, panic, condemnation, inadequacies, imperfections, and failure. People down through time also experience happiness, joy, trust, faithfulness, dedication, hope, and love. Clearly, there are ancient social practices, such as slavery, which are considered repulsive in the Western world today; yet the needs of human beings, such as freedom, seem characteristic of what it means to be a person.

An example of how human need can be explored and connected in both an ancient text and contemporary persons can be seen in Isaiah 40:27-31:

Why do you say, O Jacob,
 and speak, O Israel,
"My way is hidden from the LORD,
 and my right is disregarded by my God"?
Have you not known? Have you not heard?
The LORD is the everlasting God,
 the Creator of the ends of the earth.
He does not faint or grow weary;
 his understanding is unsearchable.

He gives power to the faint,
and strengthens the powerless.
Even youths will faint and be weary,
and the young will fall exhausted;
but those who wait for the Lord shall renew their
strength,
they shall mount up with wings like eagles,
they shall run and not be weary,
they shall walk and not faint.

This passage of Scripture comes from a period when Judah was in Babylonian exile. God's people were captive in a foreign land, without any signs that they should be optimistic about a return to their homeland. Because of this, the people questioned both God's justice and awareness. The poet reminds them that Yahweh is the creator of all reality, which is also saying that Marduk, the chief god of the Babylonians, is not. Even though the people experience exhaustion and weariness in exile, they can persevere because their hope is in Yahweh. Hope allows God to give them strength to endure the time of exile. God has not forgotten them!

What can this mean to people in the twenty-first century? Clearly, this is a proclamation to a community that lacks the resources to be optimistic. There is no conceivable way to proceed based upon the present situation. The exiled people of God are ensnared by their circumstances and cut off from the assets needed for emancipation. Therefore, they have moved to a numbing acceptance of their imprisoned condition. The question is, Are there any situations and/or human needs that bear a resemblance to this ancient state of affairs?

It should be noted that this is a communal problem, yet individuals experienced this numbing human privation. Perhaps the entrapment of many people in violent neighborhoods is an example that correlates with life lived in exile. Violence in many neighborhoods is a problem within the community itself, yet it affects the sentiments of individuals within that area. The group experiences carnage based upon a host of factors, and the community does not see a reasonable way forward to overcoming the drugs, gangs, and shootings that so often infiltrate the neighborhood. Optimism, based upon available resources, is lost.

It is into this dark and entrapped context that divine promises may be spoken. There is a way forward, but this way is based upon the Creator, who knows and cares and is able to establish a future for this community. Perhaps a new leader will emerge, much like the Persian emperor Cyrus, and the God of Israel will make a way when there seems to be no way. This biblical passage calls the reader to hope in the Creator-Redeemer God. Hope is not found in the circumstances or resources that are presently available, but in the God who speaks a promise and draws the hearer into its fulfillment. The hearer is summoned to patiently wait, and even in waiting, he or she will be given strength to fly, run, and walk!

What should be noticed about the above reflections on Isaiah 40 is that it is addressed to individuals in community. This is not a text that addresses persons who are exhausted from desiring a new job, home, or companion. This is about the exhaustion of individuals resulting from communal circumstances. When this text is applied to a privatized emotional state of mind, it may just be misappropriated. A faithful reader of the Scriptures will want to understand the situation and need of a passage in its context before associating this need with a contemporary context.

Responding to Grace

How is one to respond to the above example of Isaiah 40? Hope is the ultimate response that is called forth by this passage of Scripture. But how does one hope? Is hope an emotion? Is hope an action? If hope is the response that is desired, then what is the first thing a reader must do? Words such as "faint" and "weary" are possibly keys to unlocking the first steps in developing hope. Possibly recounting the mighty acts of God as Creator-Redeemer is the first act that a reader of this passage is called to do. Remember, hope is not optimism, but trusting in a promise made by none other than the Creator! Deuteronomy 6:12-14 is a reminder that the people of God so often forget the One who liberated them and turn to other forms of security in their everyday life and practices.

The potency of remembering the mighty acts of God both in the Scriptures and in the lives of individuals and the community itself produces a needed strength that refuses to give in to exhaustion. One could almost describe this as holding on, but this holding on is not simply hanging on in desperation. It is holding on to the God who promises a future radically different from the present situation. God will make a way where and when there seems to be no way. Most often this energy is generated within the community that reads and prays the Scriptures. Faith, hope, and love are spawned in the faith community.

Is the response of hope in the promises of God simply a matter of remembering God and refusing to give in to exhaustion? It seems that hope has one more practice within it—the practice of living into the promise. How did these exiled Jews hear this compelling promissory poem of Isaiah? It seems that at least some of them prepared to move. Living into a promise often begins with small things, but one always keeps one's eyes focused on the horizon of what is promised. If the promise is that you are going home, then pack your bags. If the promise is a neighborhood of peace and nonviolence, then begin to prepare the ground for nonaggression and peacefulness. There are children to feed and read to; there are locations available for beauty and celebration. There are poems to be written, stories to be told, and songs to be sung. God is on the move, and God's people are called to prepare to move with him. Hope can be called for as an appropriate response to a passage of Scripture, but it cannot be summoned on demand. It must be cultivated in the faith community. This same kind of cultivation can be applied to other responses: faith, love, gratitude, praise, and even obedience. Discerning the response of a pericope and imagining the steps needed to embody the response often takes time, reflection, community, and endurance.

A Theological Faith Claim

If God leaves traces of Godself in space (creation) and time (history), then why is the revelation and reality of God not apparent to so many in the world today? There are several answers that are given for why human beings are unable to discern and experience God in the world. Some of the answers are given by philosophy, culture, biology, and religion. The Bible itself addresses this baffling situation by using a variety of metaphors, such as having a hard heart or lacking eyes to see or ears to hear. The Christian tradition also describes this condition using the concept of original sin. These idioms seem to share a "family resemblance"— namely, the inability to discern the handiwork of God!

Something blocks the human creature from recognizing the presence and activity of God in space and time. The apostle Paul describes this in Romans 1:18-23:

> For the wrath of God is revealed from heaven against all ungodliness and wickedness of those who by their wickedness suppress the truth. For what can be known about God is plain to them, because God has shown it to them. Ever since the creation of the world

his eternal power and divine nature, invisible though they are, have been understood and seen through the things he has made. So they are without excuse; for though they knew God, they did not honor him as God or give thanks to him, but they became futile in their thinking, and their senseless minds were darkened. Claiming to be wise, they became fools; and they exchanged the glory of the immortal God for images resembling a mortal human being or birds or four-footed animals or reptiles.

Paul is not the only New Testament writer to address this issue. John describes this lack of awareness in the prologue of his Gospel. John 1:1-5, 10-13 states,

In the beginning was the Word, and the Word was with God, and the Word was God. He was in the beginning with God. All things came into being through him, and without him not one thing came into being. What has come into being in him was life, and the life was the light of all people. The light shines in the darkness, and the darkness did not overcome it. . . .

He was in the world, and the world came into being through him; yet the world did not know him. He came to what was his own, and his own people did not accept him. But to all who received him, who believed in his name, he gave power to become children of God, who were born, not of blood or of the will of the flesh or of the will of man, but of God.

There are many other stories and poems in the Christian Scriptures that describe this phenomenon of the inadequacy of human beings in their pursuit of understanding and in their perception of reality, but perhaps the story of the first sin in Genesis 3 is the most imposing of them all. This narrative concerns its readers with the pursuit of wisdom and the failure to recognize it. The story's setting places the first human beings in an idyllic garden with the task of caring for its welfare. Of special interest to the reader of this passage (Genesis 2:9) are two trees within the garden: "the tree of life also in the midst of the garden, and the tree of the knowledge of good and evil." It is obvious to the reader that the "tree of the knowledge of good and evil" is about the perception of reality and its values, but what does the "tree of life" represent? What did it mean to the ancient people of God? Is this tree and its fruit something that has a type of magical or mysterious influence upon those who eat of it? Or is it also addressing the issue of the perception of reality and thus values? A possible answer may come from the wisdom tradition in ancient Israel. In this tradition, the "tree of life" is a metaphor for wisdom herself. Proverbs 3:18 states, "She is a tree of life to those who lay hold of her; those who hold her fast are called happy." Wisdom is not only a way of life but the way to life. In the standard wisdom tradition, two ways are open to human beings: the way of folly and the way of wisdom. To pursue wisdom is to pursue life, but the way of the fool is the way of death. Whatever this concept is attempting to communicate in the story, the results of the ongoing narrative are clear: misperception, competition, faultfinding, misunderstanding, and ever-increasing violence. In other words, eating from the "tree of the knowledge of good and evil" leads to death!

If human beings are unable to perceive God's activity in space and time, then how can they read the Scriptures as a lens to recognize God in creation and history? This quandary is made extremely evident in Israel's response to the coming of God in the person of Jesus. Israel was a recipient of election, liberation, land, the temple, and even the Scriptures, yet they rejected the coming of God in Christ. Jesus was not recognized as the Messiah, but as a blasphemer and a threat to all that is holy. If devoted readers of the Torah and the Prophets did not recognize God's presence in Jesus, then is it even remotely probable that casual and apathetic readers of the Scriptures today will recognize the world as God's world?

The New Testament bears witnesses to the fact that Jesus was overwhelmingly opposed by some of the most religious persons of the first century. The parable of the soils in Mark 4 displays a pattern of response to the word of God's kingdom. In this parable there are four types of soils: the path (represented by the religious), rocky ground (represented by the disciples), thorns (represented by the rich young ruler and Pilate), and good soil (represented by the masses of needy people). Although there is not space to explore the literary character of Mark's Gospel in the light of this parable, it should be noted that these soils represent the various responses to the kingdom of God. The first two responses (soils) expose misperceptions of the intention of God's reign. The religious persons of first-century Jerusalem were already so habituated that they could not recognize the presence of God in Jesus. The disciples recognized the presence of God in Jesus, but their preconceived beliefs anticipated something very different from what Jesus intended. Thorny soil represents persons who are able to perceive the good news of the kingdom of God; yet the cares and values of the present age keep them from appropriating the rule and reign of God. Finally, those who have little to nothing in this present age are the good soil. They have little to lose and everything to gain in the kingdom of God. The question contemporary readers need to ask, in the light of this parable, is, How is it possible to read the Bible as a lens through which one is able to see to ways of God in creation and history while being habituated by this present age and its beliefs and values? Surely it will take a miracle—the miracle of God's Spirit and grace—to make the blind see, the deaf hear, and the lame leap like deer.

How does God, Godself, enable the inspirational moment of reading the Bible? This question presupposes the ongoing activity of God revealing Godself through the Scriptures. The faith claim of this book on how to read the Bible Christianly is that the same Spirit that opened the eyes of the first responders to God's activity and enabled the long history of the traditioning process is the same Spirit that is operative in the faith community today. This does not mean that the canon of Scripture should be open, but that the same God who is witnessed to in the Scriptures is the God who is present to the believing community. God reveals Godself as Godself by means of Godself! This mystery of the self-disclosure of God is not simply something for reading but also for living. Truly the Bible witnesses to God's activity, but it also communicates to its readers something about the world. The world is none other than God's world. By the inspiration of God's own Spirit, the reader is given ears to hear and eyes to see. Matthew's Gospel says it well: "But blessed are your eyes, for they see, and your ears, for they hear" (13:16).

Embodying the Text

Many who are reading this book have participated in events such youth camps and/or mission trips. What is interesting is that many people perceive a closer encounter with God during these intense times. The problem is that within a few weeks, after returning to their old forms of life, their perception of God's presence and activity dims. They have withdrawn from the intensity of Bible studies, worship, and passionate spiritual relationships in which they briefly participated. Often, on returning home, they believe things will be different, but with the passing of time and the changing of patterns, they return to their old cycles and practices. The question that this chapter is attempting to answer is not how people can keep alive an enthusiastic passion, such as that experienced on a mission trip, but how biblical readers can become so engaged in the Scriptures that the discernment of God's presence and purpose captivates and transforms their very characters.

The premise of this book on how to read the Bible Christianly is that human beings are linguistically construed. This means that people dwell in language systems or communities of memory. Because there are different language systems or forms of life, there are different ways that these cultural-linguistic frameworks interpret the world and function within the world. These linguistic systems are shared by groups of language users designated in this book as communities of memory; therefore, one could say that there is no private language. Communities of memory have rules they operate within, in much the same way as a language has a grammar. Individuals learn these linguistic arrangements or rules primarily by participating with others in communal practices and storytelling. The stories told are not simply random but are a part of a larger language tapestry or worldview that emerges from and contributes to a grand narrative. These grand narratives endeavor to describe the world; they have beginnings, and they are moving toward an anticipated end or a good to be pursued. Therefore, as individuals are shaped by a grand narrative, they find themselves participating in the narrative as characters in a story. Persons live within these narrative worlds and embody the beliefs, values, and goals of these worlds.

Ancient Israelites were no different. They told stories and understood reality from a place—their story-formed world of Yahweh's creative and redemptive action in creation. The beliefs of their storytellers, prophets, and poets, as well as the convictions constituting the premise of this book on reading the Bible, understood that God leaves traces of Godself in space and time. God's self-disclosure takes place in creation and history. What the argument of this essay is making is that this self-disclosure of God is interpreted from the existing linguistic frameworks of ancient Israel across time. Therefore, the narrative world of the biblical texts is developing in the course of events. This enlarging and illuminating of the story is what is described as the process of a developing tradition.

As outlined earlier, by the early first century, the grand narrative went something like this: There is one God who created everything that exists. The Creator has chosen a people, Israel, to represent and reflect him to the rest of creation. He rescued the people from Egyptian bondage and gifted them with both a land of promise and his will in the form of Torah. Because they failed to reflect the Creator's character, they once again found themselves strangers and exiles, removed from the land of promise. But the Creator was not finished with them; they were rescued and reconstituted and given the promise that creation itself would be remade to reflect the will of the Creator. This hope was nothing less than restoring the reign of the Creator and humanity as his emissary.

It was into this story-formed world that Jesus the Messiah was born. He was also shaped by this grand narrative and yet brought a distinctive understanding to the reign of God. His singular message was nothing less than the gospel of the kingdom of God is at hand! This message was proclaimed and embodied by him in many ways. Those who responded to him were told to leave their linguistic worlds, with all of their practices, stories, and values, and follow him. Their lives would enter into an altogether different world through baptism, and they were to "walk in newness of life." Romans 6:4 says this well: "Therefore we have been buried with him by baptism into death, so that, just as Christ was raised from the dead by the glory of the Father, so we too might walk in newness of life."

If Christian faith is dependent upon hearing the good, gleeful, glad tidings of the gospel of God in Jesus the Messiah, and if this hearing of God's story of reconciliation and renewal of creation is assumed by faith, then God's grace appropriated by the miracle of faith will transfigure believers into God's grand story. Listen to the words of Ephesians 2:8: "For by grace you have been saved through faith, and this is not your own doing; it is the gift of God." If persons of faith are going to read the Bible Christianly, then they will be apprehended by the story-formed world they are reading. This sort of reading summons its readers to partici-

To see the world as God's world is an interpretive task that requires a new language, with new ears to hear and eyes to see. It requires a new people who are raised in newness of life.

pate in the ongoing narrative of God's creative and redemptive activity in the world. This chapter will explore what it means to embody the Bible and how this embodiment happens in the lives of believers.

What Embodying Scripture Means

Before exploring the *what* and the *how* of embodying Scripture, a few words need to be said about what this embodiment does not mean. First, embodying the Scripture does not mean a legalistic approach to Scripture. A new covenant community of memory is reminded in the Scriptures themselves that legalism or the law kills. The transformation of human character is brought about very differently. Paul writes in 2 Corinthians 3:4-6: "Such is the confidence that we have through Christ toward God. Not that we are competent of ourselves to claim anything as coming from us; our competence is from God, who has made us competent to be ministers of a new covenant, not of letter but of spirit; for the letter kills, but the Spirit gives life." A Christian community of memory is not called to woodenly perform the words found in select passages of the Bible, but to become participants in the ongoing interpreted and interpreting story of God in God's new creation.

Second, embodying Scripture means that participating in the ongoing story of God is at least an interpretive task. Faithful readers of Scripture do not have to abandon their intellect to faithfully participate in the biblical plot of God's rescue and restoration of creation. Forcing a pseudo belief in an ancient cosmology is not a necessary condition for the faithful Christian reading of Scripture. A person can be a scientist, a historian, and even a philosopher and remain an embodied follower of Jesus Christ. But embodying the Scriptures does insinuate that God is the creator of the heavens and the earth and that God is on the way, with his people, toward rescue, reconciliation, and restoration of all of creation. To see the world as God's world is an interpretive task that requires a new language, with new ears to hear and eyes to see. It requires a new people who are raised in newness of life.

Becoming a participant in the unfolding story of God's rescue mission of creation is the goal of embodying the Scripture. To be a participant in the mission of God necessitates new eyes to see and new ears to hear; it requires the transformation of human character. This conversion becomes the humanly unachievable challenge of reading the Bible Christianly. Only God can enable this new reality! To read the Bible Christianly is founded upon being a Christian, and being a Christian is to participate in the grand story of God's redemptive mission of all of creation.

How Embodying Scripture Happens

The *zeitgeist*, the defining spirit of the times, in every period of history mitigates the power of the Bible in and for the world. In other words, there is an eclipse of the biblical narrative where even the Bible is used in the service of the spirit of the time. This eclipse results in a famine of spiritual and moral imagination for the sake of the world. Fear and desire govern this present, spiritless aeon, and the result is a loss of meaning and purpose. The characteristics of this age are superficiality and restlessness. Speed and impulse drive this present age, and meditating, praying, Bible reading, and imagining are forgotten practices from long ago and far away. Anything that requires time and diligence produces the greatest rancor. When "drive through dining" and "instant data" are the norm, then the time required to become a saint must be reduced and sainthood itself must be redefined. What can be done? How can the people of God enter into a second naïveté?

Perhaps it is time to return to a few of the ancient practices in order to recover the language of the people of God. One possible practice is a return to the *lectio divina*. This is a Benedictine practice that literally means "divine reading." The *lectio divina* has five basic steps: reading, meditation, prayer, contemplation, and action. This chapter is going to modify and reorder these steps and redescribe them as reading the Bible, praying the Scriptures, theological reflection within the world, confession, and enacting the text.

Reading the Bible

Most persons in the twenty-first century listen to and are shaped by alternative narratives with their beliefs and value systems. Seldom do these stories reflect the narrative world of God's creative and redemptive work. All too often the Bible is read simply as a footnote to reinforce an alien narrative worldview. Contemporary persons are inundated by these story-formed worlds that not only do not reflect God's story but are antithetical to its values and purpose. Given the reality of these conflicting story-formed worlds, how are present-day readers of the Bible to read with a second naïveté? There are at least three aspects of reading the Bible that are necessary if a person is going to be engrafted into its story: reading the Bible as a whole narrative, reading the Bible closely within a passage, and reading the Bible in community.

Reading the Bible as a Whole Narrative. Individual passages of Scripture find their meaning in context. These contexts are multifaceted, as was discussed in previous chapters, but the context implied here is that of the whole story of God as told by Israel and the early Christian community. It is in this context that individual passages make their contributions. It should always be remembered that the Christian Bible points to and from the gospel of the kingdom of God as it was announced, was embodied, was initiated, and will be finally completed in Jesus the Messiah. This means that unique attention must be given to the life of Jesus as attested in the Gospels of Matthew, Mark, Luke, and John. The only description of Jesus that Christians have is that narrated in the Gospels. This does not mean that the Old Testament and the remainder of the New Testament are of no value or even lesser value. They are written witnesses to the self-disclosure of God that is fulfilled in Jesus the Messiah. Old Testament stories find their fulfillment in Jesus the Messiah, and the New Testament letters are understood as witnesses to the self-disclosure of God in the life, death, resurrection, and ascension of Jesus and the outpouring of the Holy Spirit. The Christ event is at the heart of a Christian understanding of the story of God as witnessed to in the Sacred Scriptures. But to understand the Christ event itself, one must read the whole Bible.

Reading the whole of Scripture is a daunting task, especially in a culture that puts a premium on speed and brevity. The Bible is a long and strange book. It is written in languages that are not the mother tongues of the readers, who possess different worldviews and even value systems. A further challenge is in the reader. Many churchgoing persons are more engaged and therefore influenced by social media, pop culture, and sporting events than they are by the reading of the sacred texts. Therefore, the Scripture is read through the lens of the controlling narrative worldview of the reader. It is only in reading, rereading, and then reading again the Bible in its entirety that one even begins to understand the plot of the strange new world of God's story. As one can imagine, this takes time, discipline, and accountability. It also requires a strategy.

There are several strategies for reading the Bible. Some readers begin with the book of Genesis and do not stop until they finish with the book of Revelation. At some period in one's life, this approach is very beneficial. Another tactic is to attempt to read the Scriptures in a historical manner. This is especially helpful in reading the prophetic texts. When a reader is able to place the material in chronological order, it lends perspective to the books being read. This will also involve reading scholarly introductions to the Bible and will enable a reader to develop a tethered imagination. Another suggestion is to use an aid to guide one's reading of the Bible. These aids can be the Daily Office or similar Bible reading handbooks. A final resource for Scripture reading can be a Bible designed to be read in its entirety in a year. All of these biblical-spiritual resources have been used by this author, and the use of the Daily Office, along with the *Revised Common Lectionary*, has proven most useful. Whatever strategy is employed, reading the whole Bible to understand its plenary message is essential if one is going to become a performer in the grand narrative-drama of God's redemption and rescue of creation.

Reading the Bible Closely within a Passage. It takes time not only to read the Bible as a whole but also to read it closely in its individual parts. Not much space will be given to describing this close reading, because this book on how to read the Bible Christianly is designed to demonstrate how to read these ancient texts closely. Contexts must be understood, structures need to be appreciated, words and concepts must be comprehended, and beliefs about God and his world ought to be recognized. It is in this close reading of a passage of Scripture that its message is released to encounter the reader. This encounter is when the text itself begins to read the reader. Remember that the reader is also story formed.

Reading the Bible in Community. No individual can read well enough or live long enough to be swallowed up by the biblical story on his or her own. It takes a community of readers to read the Bible well. This kinship of readers consists of the community of faith and its historical scholarship. One might ask, Why does reading the Bible well require a community of faith and learning? The answer to this is at least threefold: First, the Christian Bible is the church's book. Second, akin to what was just stated, no one lives long enough or reads well enough to comprehend the whole of Scripture on his or her own. Third, to embody the story witnessed to in Scripture requires a community of memory whose members can tell the stories of faith to one another, practice in their communal life the Scriptures, become exemplars for one another and the world of the embodied beliefs and values of the Bible, and cultivate and transmit the ancient symbols of Christian identity.

There is a children's song with the following lyrics:

Jesus loves me! this I know,
For the Bible tells me so.
Little ones to Him belong;
They are weak, but He is strong.

Yes, Jesus loves me.
Yes, Jesus loves me.
Yes, Jesus loves me.
The Bible tells me so.[1]

Perhaps the song should have one more line to make it complete: "And the church tells me that the Bible is telling the truth." Why is this extra line a part of the story of the Bible? Because the Bible not only belongs to the church but also is a product of the witness of God's people to his revelation in space and time. Therefore, the Bible comes from the church and confronts the church. It is the identi-

---

1. Anna B. Warner and William B. Bradbury, "Jesus Loves Me," 1860-62, in *Sing to the Lord* (Kansas City: Lillenas, 1993), no. 738.

ty-forming document of God's people, and it witnesses to their story as God's own story.

If reading Scripture in community is to happen at all, it needs to occur in worship. All too often in evangelical congregations the focus of worship is placed upon music, commitment, or the sermon, which can be taken from a variety of narrative worlds. Congregants often respond to the service of worship with comments such as, "I like the music," or "That's not my kind of music." Many congregants will respond to the sermon as it communicates helpfulness or the lack of helpfulness to their lives. Often this helpfulness and their lives are based upon other narrative worlds within which they find their own identities. The strange narrative world of the Bible is eclipsed by other narrative worlds and their values. Parishioners are often locked out of the Bible's story-formed world and are left to repair the false worlds they inhabit with only fragments and phrases from the Bible. If communities of memory are going to inhabit the strange new world of God's story-formed kingdom, then the Bible will need to be read well and for longer periods in worship. If it is not read in worship, then why would anyone believe it should be read with seriousness at any other time or place?

Reading Scripture in community involves reading the Bible not only with the living but also with the dead. This does not mean having some sort of mystical experience with the dead, but participating in the resources of the dead for the living. Reading the Bible with the saints and scholars of the past allows the present-day reader to utilize the resources of past reflection, prayer, and scholarship. Remember, it takes more than a lifetime to apprehend the story of God. This does not mean that God is not writing readers into the narrative of rescue and redemption, but that the meaning of the story must be told and understood down through history. Present-day readers of the Bible are participants in the Christian heritage. The labors of Christian scholars and saints create understanding of both the larger canonical story and its smaller parts.

When one reads the Bible Christianly, the reader is rewritten into its story. This embodiment within the story of God, along with the embodiment of the story of God within the individual reader, is an ethical movement. This type of ethics is not about knowing the right thing to do in such and such a situation, but about becoming the right kind of person for all situations. It is about becoming a person of Christian character, a saint. The habits of the heart are reformed in such a way that a person can honestly say that he or she is a new person, a new creation. How is this possible? Clearly this is the work of the Spirit of God that dwells in and through the Christian community. The Christian community, with its practices, stories, exemplars, and symbols, is a means of grace through which the Spirit can work in the transformational process. It takes a community of saints to raise an individual saint. Holiness is caught by the virus of grace administered by the Spirit through the communion of saints.

Praying the Scriptures

The argument so far is that reading the Bible Christianly implies that transformation takes place in the lives of readers. This conversion is recognized in both the Bible and Christian tradition as the work of God's Spirit. The question now is how does the Spirit work in and through the reading of Scripture? If the Bible is read basically to ask questions of history, then the answers will merely be historical. If the Bible is read solely to explore the literary makeup of a passage, then only the literary makeup of a passage will be discovered. If the Bible is read in longing for God, then prayer will become an irreplaceable component in the yearning to know God. The historical Christian community developed a collection of phrases: *Lex orandi, lex credendi, lex vivendi.* (Latin, "The law of praying is the law of believing is the law of living.")

If the transformation of character is the desired outcome of Christianly reading the Bible, then God's Spirit and grace are necessary. One cannot simply make oneself believe something is true any more than one can force oneself to be different. The above Latin phrase implies that what one is Christianly is a result of what one believes, and what one believes is made possible by the Spirit within the Christian community. The concept of prayer implies the presence of the Other known as God. When a reader of the Bible studies in prayer, he or she presupposes that the God witnessed to in the Scriptures is present in his or her reading. He or she is praying for discernment.

Theological Reflection within the World

How is one to describe this discernment? There are at least three questions—two concerning God and one the reader(s)—that are essential to discern in and through every passage of Scripture:

1. Who are you?
2. Where are you?
3. What are we to do?

First, the question of who God is not only should be explored in the text but also searched for in the reader's world. God is disclosed in space and time and continues to work in creation and history. Perhaps the phrase to continually pray in the presence of God is, "Lord, give us eyes to see you in your world."

The second question to ask in the prayer for discernment is, Where are you? It should be remembered that every text emerges from a human dilemma or need.

Tethered by the biblical text, prayer liberates the purpose of God to create an imagination born of the Spirit for the world.

Though situations change from ancient periods of time to the present, there is a family resemblance to human need. God, as witnessed to in the biblical text, is engaged with the destitute in creation. Where is God? God is with the deprivation of humanity. The same God witnessed to in the text is working in the twenty-first century. Where are the cries that are going up to God? Cries of injustice, deficiency, denial, sin, and despair? Perhaps the phrase to continually pray in the presence of God is, "Lord, give us ears to hear the anguish of creation."

The final question to ask in the prayer for discernment is, What are we to do? In the previous chapter, this question was discussed at great length, but a few comments may prove helpful. First, the biblical text will instruct the reader in the appropriate response. A few examples may be helpful concerning the call a passage of Scripture directs to its readers. If the biblical text is a command or imperative, then obedience to the charge of God is mandated. What is helpful to understand is that the response is to God and God's directive. In other words, it is a response to the activity of God. Another example can be observed in the type of genre being read. If one is reading a thanksgiving psalm, then repentance or even obedience is not the directive. The exhortation is to give thanks. A final example is a narrative of God's saving activity toward the weak or marginalized. This example can have at least two possible responses based upon the position of the reader. If the reader is weak and marginalized, then trust that God is moving to rescue seems appropriate. If the reader is in a position of strength, then discerning the work of God on behalf of the marginalized and cooperating with the movement of God is appropriate.

Prayerful readers of the Scriptures listen with ears of grace and see with eyes of compassion the needy in the world. Tethered by the biblical text, prayer liberates the purpose of God to create an imagination born of the Spirit for the world. The Christian community and individual disciples are called to enact the text in their space and time. This listening and seeing in prayer creates a tethered imagination to engage the world that God created and is redeeming.

Confession

An imagination birthed by the Spirit calls for not only performance but also confession. "To confess" in the Greek language is the word *homologeō*. This word literally means "to speak the same" and is a response to a prior speaking—namely, the speaking of the Spirit through the biblical passage. To confess, or speak the same, is to acknowledge the Spirit's inspiration through the pericope to the prayerful reader. In inspiration, the text is God's very speaking or disclosure to the present-day reader. It is God's Word!

Often confession is to speak to the truth about who God is and what God is doing. By this act of confession, faith is working in both the community and the individual disciple. At other times, the work of the Spirit through the biblical text brings awareness to the community and individual disciple that they are out of step with the purpose and will of God. In these times, confession is acknowledging the difference between God's intention and the reality of the form of life the community of disciples is living. First John 1:5-10 is a powerful reminder of the work of God in the community of faith:

> This is the message we have heard from him and proclaim to you, that God is light and in him there is no darkness at all. If we say that we have fellowship with him while we are walking in darkness, we lie and do not do what is true; but if we walk in the light as he himself is in the light, we have fellowship with one another, and the blood of Jesus his Son cleanses us from all sin. If we say that we have no sin, we deceive

ourselves, and the truth is not in us. If we confess our sins, he who is faithful and just will forgive us our sins and cleanse us from all unrighteousness. If we say that we have not sinned, we make him a liar, and his word is not in us.

Confession can be painful when one faces doubts and failures, but in the practice of confession, God enables liberation and transformation. Perhaps the beginning of confession is found in the humble words "Lord, have mercy; Christ, have mercy,"[2] or possibly it is the words of the father, recorded in Mark 9:24, who asked for help: "I believe; help my unbelief!" By implication, confession recognizes the world as God's world.

Enacting the Text

Reading the Bible Christianly is never complete until faithful readers see their world as God's world. This means that the goal for readers of the Bible is to see, feel, and act in the world as participants in the story of God. James 1:22-25 says just as much:

> But be doers of the word, and not merely hearers who deceive themselves. For if any are hearers of the word and not doers, they are like those who look at themselves in a mirror; for they look at themselves and, on going away, immediately forget what they were like. But those who look into the perfect law, the law of liberty, and persevere, being not hearers who forget but doers who act—they will be blessed in their doing.

The story of God, as witnessed to in Scripture, shapes a form of life that summons its readers as participants in that very story.

---

2. *The Book of Common Prayer* (New York: Seabury Press, 1979), 132.

This is not an order to simply add religious vocabulary or even stories to a present narrative world, but to so participate in the language system of the Man from heaven that the very perceptions and affections of the community and its disciples are transformed. It is nothing less than having a new mind, the mind of Christ (Phil. 2:5). It also involves resistance to this present age and its narrative form of life, and it beckons its readers to give themselves over to the vision of the new-age kingdom of God (Rom. 12:1-2). It is daily leaving the narrative world of this present aeon and following Christ the proclaimer, embodiment, and initiator of the new-age kingdom of God (Luke 9:23). The disclosure of God's voice is not an addition to the present state of affairs, but an invitation to a new world order.

What are the virtues that will allow a reader of the Bible to become a participant in its story? The central virtues of early Christianity can be seen in the apostle Paul's declaration in 1 Corinthians 13:9-13:

> For we know only in part, and we prophesy only in part; but when the complete comes, the partial will come to an end. When I was a child, I spoke like a child, I thought like a child, I reasoned like a child; when I became an adult, I put an end to childish ways. For now we see in a mirror, dimly, but then we will see face to face. Now I know only in part; then I will know fully, even as I have been fully known. And now faith, hope, and love abide, these three; and the greatest of these is love.

Faith, hope, and love are the virtues that Paul articulates as lasting. Trust in the God who is disclosed uniquely in Jesus the Messiah, and live into his future as one's own future, and love him and one's neighbor—even one's enemy!

These virtues are transparent and straight forward, yet they take a lifetime of living in faithful community to habituate. One cannot know whom to trust unless one hears the story and its stories over and over again. One cannot develop the moral muscle memory to act Christianly unless one repetitively participates in the practices of the new age of God's kingdom; worship, hospitality, and nonviolence take a lifetime of living in faithful community to habituate. One cannot imagine what a faithful character in the story of God looks like unless there are exemplars, both past and present, to show the way of citizenship in the kingdom of God. One cannot be drawn into the milieu of the story unless one is captivated over and over again through the symbols of the kingdom: the cross, the body of Christ, the sacraments, the mission of God, and the Book! There are many imposters who speak with the vocabulary of the people of God but do so through the grammar of this present age and its false narratives.

Second Timothy 3:1-5, 14-17 is a warning to the twenty-first-century church:

> You must understand this, that in the last days distressing times will come. For people will be lovers of themselves, lovers of money, boasters, arrogant, abusive, disobedient to their parents, ungrateful, unholy, inhuman, implacable, slanderers, profligates, brutes, haters of good, treacherous, reckless, swollen with conceit, lovers of pleasure rather than lovers of God, holding to the outward form of godliness but denying its power. Avoid them! . . .
>
> . . . But as for you, continue in what you have learned and firmly believed, knowing from whom you learned it, and how from childhood you have known the sacred writings that are able to instruct you for salvation through faith in Christ Jesus. All scripture is inspired by God and is useful for teaching, for reproof, for correction, and for training in righteousness, so

that everyone who belongs to God may be proficient, equipped for every good work.

The Bible intends to draw those who read its pages, believe its witness, and enact its story into the strange new world of God's redemptive kingdom. It is perhaps then that a reader will not simply understand this strange new world but be comprehended by it. After finishing the argument of this book, you might be saying to yourself, dear reader, that the task is beyond your capacity to undertake. Possibly you need to begin with a prayer:

Lord, have mercy; Christ, have mercy.

I believe, help my unbelief.

Bibliography

Alt, Albrecht. "The Origins of Israelite Law." In *Essays on Old Testament History and Religion*, 101-71. Garden City: Doubleday, 1968.

Alter, Robert. *The Art of Biblical Narrative*. New York: Basic Books, 1981.

Anderson, Bernhard W. *Understanding the Old Testament*. 4th ed. Englewood Cliffs, NJ: Prentice-Hall, 1986.

Anscombe, G. E. M. *Ethics, Religion, and Politics*. Oxford, UK: Basil Blackwell, 1981.

Austin, J. L. *How to Do Things with Words*. Oxford, UK: Clarendon Press, 1962.

———. *Sense and Sensibilia*. Oxford, UK: Clarendon Press, 1962.

Barth, Karl. *Church Dogmatics I.1*. London: T and T Clark, 1975.

———. *Church Dogmatics I.2*. London: T and T Clark, 1956.

———. *Church Dogmatics II.2*. London: T and T Clark, 1957.

———. *Dogmatics in Outline*. New York: Harper and Row, 1959.

———. *The Word of God and the Word of Man*. Gloucester, MA: Peter Smith, 1978.

Bartor, Assnat. *Reading Law as Narrative: A Study in the Casuistic Laws of the Pentateuch*. Atlanta: Society of Biblical Literature, 2010.

Bell, Daniel M., Jr. *Liberation Theology after the End of History: The Refusal to Cease Suffering*. London: Routledge, 2001.

Berger, Peter, and Thomas Luckmann. *The Social Construction of Reality: A Treatise in the Sociology of Knowledge*. New York: Anchor Books, 1966.

Bonhoeffer, Dietrich. *The Cost of Discipleship*. London: SCM Press, 1959. Reprint, New York: Touchstone, 1995.

Borg, Marcus J. *Conflict, Holiness, and Politics in the Teachings of Jesus*. New York: E. Mellen, 1984.

———. *The Heart of Christianity: Rediscovering a Life of Faith*. New York: HarperCollins, 2004.

Bourdieu, Pierre. *Outline of a Theory of Practice*. Cambridge, UK: Cambridge University Press, 2018.

Bratcher, Robert G., and Howard A. Hatton. *A Handbook on Deuteronomy*. New York: United Bible Societies, 2000.

Brueggemann, Walter. *The Land: Place as Gift, Promise, and Challenge in Biblical Faith*. Minneapolis: Fortress Press, 1977.

———. *Old Testament Theology: An Introduction*. Nashville: Abingdon Press, 2008.

———. *Theology of the Old Testament: Testimony, Dispute, Advocacy*. Minneapolis: Fortress Press, 1997.

Buber, Martin. *I and Thou*. Mansfield Centre, CT: Martino, 2010.

———. *Kingship of God*. New York: Harper and Row, 1967.

Campbell, Antony F., and Mark A. O'Brien. *Unfolding the Deuteronomistic History: Origins, Upgrades, Present Text*. Minneapolis: Augsburg Fortress, 2000.

Campbell, Ted A. *The Gospel in Christian Traditions*. Oxford, UK: Oxford University Press, 2009.

Chaney, Marvin L. "Debt Easement in Israelite History and Tradition." In *The Bible and the Politics of Exegesis*, edited by David Jobling, Peggy L. Day, and Gerald T. Sheppard, 127-39. Cleveland: Pilgrim Press, 1991.

Childs, Brevard S. *The Book of Exodus: A Critical, Theological Commentary*. Old Testament Library. Louisville, KY: Westminster John Knox Press, 1974.

———. *Memory and Tradition in Israel*. London: SCM Press, 1962.

———. *Old Testament Theology in a Canonical Context*. Philadelphia: Fortress Press, 1985.

Crenshaw, James L., ed. *Theodicy in the Old Testament*. Philadelphia: Fortress Press, 1983.

Davies, E. W. "Land: Its Rights and Privileges." In *The World of Ancient Israel: Sociological, Anthropological, and Political Perspectives*, edited by R. E. Clements, 349-69. Cambridge, UK: Cambridge University Press, 1991.

Donner, Herbert. "The Separate States of Israel and Judah." In *Israelite and Judaean History*, edited by John H. Hayes and J. Maxwell Miller. London: SCM Press, 1990.

Doorly, William J. *Obsession with Justice: The Story of the Deuteronomists*. New York: Paulist Press, 1994.

Dulles, Avery. *Models of Revelation*. New York: Doubleday, 1983.

Dunn, James. *Beginning from Jerusalem*. Grand Rapids: Eerdmans, 2009.

———. *Jesus Remembered*. Grand Rapids: Eerdmans, 2003.

———. *Neither Jew nor Greek*. Grand Rapids: Eerdmans, 2015.

Fishbane, Michael. *The Garments of Torah: Essays in Biblical Hermeneutics*. Bloomington, IN: Indiana University Press, 1989.

Frei, Hans. *The Eclipse of Biblical Narrative: A Study in Eighteenth and Nineteenth Century Hermeneutics*. New Haven, CT: Yale University Press, 1974.

———. *The Identity of Jesus Christ: The Hermeneutical Bases of Dogmatic Theology*. Philadelphia: Fortress Press, 1975.

———. *Theology and Narrative: Selected Essays*. Edited by George Hunsinger and William C. Placher. New York: Oxford University Press, 1993.

———. *Types of Christian Theology*. Edited by George Hunsinger and William C. Placher. New Haven, CT: Yale University Press, 1992.

Fretheim, Terence. *God and World in the Old Testament: A Relational Theology of Creation*. Nashville: Abingdon Press, 2005.

———. "The Repentance of God: A Key to Evaluating Old Testament God-Talk." *Horizons in Biblical Theology* 10, no. 1 (1988): 47-70.

Gadamer, Hans-Georg. *Truth and Method*. 2nd ed. New York: Continuum, 1994.

Garver, Newton. *This Complicated Form of Life: Essays on Wittgenstein*. Chicago: Open Court, 1994.

Geertz, Clifford. *The Interpretation of Cultures*. New York: Basic Books, 1977.

Green, Timothy M. *The God Plot: Living with Holy Imagination*. Kansas City: Beacon Hill Press of Kansas City, 2014.

Habel, Norman C. *The Land Is Mine: Six Biblical Land Ideologies*. Minneapolis: Fortress Press, 1995.

Hanson, Paul D. *The People Called: The Growth of Community in the Bible*. San Francisco: Harper and Row, 1986.

Harrelson, Walter. "Life, Faith, and the Emergence of Tradition." In *Tradition and Theology in the Old Testament*, edited by Douglas A. Knight, 11-30. Philadelphia: Fortress Press, 1977.

———. *The Ten Commandments and Human Rights*. Macon, GA: Mercer University Press, 1997.

Hauerwas, Stanley. *A Community of Character: Toward a Constructive Christian Social Ethic*. Notre Dame, IN: University of Notre Dame Press, 1981.

———. *The Peaceable Kingdom: A Primer in Christian Ethics*. Notre Dame, IN: University of Notre Dame Press, 1983.

Hauerwas, Stanley, and L. Gregory Jones, eds. *Why Narrative? Readings in Narrative Theology*. Grand Rapids: Eerdmans, 1989.

Heidegger, Martin. *Being and Time*. London: SCM Press, 1962.

Henry, Carl F. H. *God Who Speaks and Shows: Preliminary Considerations*. Vol. 1 of *God, Revelation and Authority*. Waco, TX: Word Books, 1976.

Heschel, Abraham. *Man Is Not Alone: A Philosophy of Religion*. New York: Harper and Row, 1951.

High, Dallas M. *Language, Persons, and Belief*. New York: Oxford University Press, 1967.

Hollinger, Robert, ed. *Hermeneutics and Praxis*. Notre Dame, IN: University of Notre Dame Press, 1985.

Holmer, Paul L. *The Grammar of Faith*. New York: Harper and Row, 1978.

———. *Making Christian Sense: Spirituality and the Christian Life*. Philadelphia: Westminster Press, 1984.

Houston, Walter J. *Contending for Justice: Ideologies and Theologies of Social Justice in the Old Testament*. New York: T and T Clark, 2006.

Jenson, Robert W. *Canon and Creed*. Interpretation: Resources for the Use of Scripture in the Church. Louisville, KY: Westminster John Knox Press, 2010.

———. *The Triune God*. Vol. 1 of *Systematic Theology*. New York: Oxford University Press, 1997.

———. *The Works of God*. Vol. 2 of *Systematic Theology*. New York: Oxford University Press, 1999.

Jones, L. Gregory. *Embodying Forgiveness: A Theological Analysis*. Grand Rapids: Eerdmans, 1995.

Knight, Douglas A. *Law, Power, and Justice in Ancient Israel*. Louisville, KY: Westminster John Knox Press, 2011.

Knight, George A. F. *Theology as Narration: A Commentary on the Book of Exodus*. Grand Rapids: Eerdmans, 1976.

Lindbeck, George. *The Nature of Doctrine*. Louisville, KY: Westminster John Knox Press, 1984.

Long, D. Stephen. *Speaking of God: Theology, Language, and Truth*. Grand Rapids: Eerdmans, 2009.

———. *Theology and Culture: A Guide to the Discussion*. Eugene, OR: Cascade Companions, 2008.

MacIntyre, Alasdair. *After Virtue: A Study in Moral Theory*. Notre Dame, IN: University of Notre Dame Press, 1981.

———. *Three Rival Versions of Moral Enquiry*. Notre Dame, IN: University of Notre Dame Press, 1990.

———. *Whose Justice? Which Rationality?* Notre Dame, IN: University of Notre Dame Press, 1988.

McClendon, James Wm., Jr. *Doctrine*. Vol. 2 of *Systematic Theology*. Nashville: Abingdon Press, 1994.

———. *Ethics*. Vol. 1 of *Systematic Theology*. Nashville: Abingdon Press, 1986.

———. *Witness*. Vol. 3 of *Systematic Theology*. Nashville: Abingdon Press, 2000.

McClendon, James Wm., Jr., and James M. Smith. *Understanding Religious Convictions*. Notre Dame, IN: University of Notre Dame Press, 1975.

McFague, Sallie. *Metaphorical Theology: Models of God in Religious Language*. Philadelphia: Fortress Press, 1982.

———. *Speaking in Parables: A Study in Metaphor and Theology*. Philadelphia: Fortress Press, 1975.

Mendenhall, George E. *Law and Covenant in Israel and the Ancient Near East*. Pittsburgh: Biblical Colloquium, 1955.

———. *The Tenth Generation: The Origins of the Biblical Tradition*. Baltimore: Johns Hopkins University Press, 1973.

Milbank, John. *Theology and Social Theory: Beyond Secular Reason*. Oxford, UK: Blackwell, 1990.

Miller, Patrick D. *The Ten Commandments*. Interpretation: Resources for the Use of Scripture in the Church. Louisville, KY: Westminster John Knox Press, 2009.

Murphy, Nancey. *Anglo-American Postmodernity: Philosophical Perspectives on Science, Religion, and Ethics*. Boulder, CO: Westview Press, 1997.

———. *Beyond Liberalism and Fundamentalism: How Modern and Postmodern Philosophy Set the Theological Agenda*. Valley Forge, PA: Trinity Press International, 1996.

Niebuhr, H. Richard. *The Meaning of Revelation*. New York: Macmillan, 1941.

Nugent, John C. *The Politics of Yahweh: John Howard Yoder, the Old Testament, and the People of God*. Eugene, OR: Cascade Books, 2011.

Olson, Dennis T. *Deuteronomy and the Death of Moses: A Theological Reading*. Minneapolis: Augsburg Fortress Press, 1994.

Pannenberg, Wolfhart. *Revelation as History*. New York: Macmillan, 1968.

Phillips, D. Z. *The Concept of Prayer*. New York: Seabury Press, 1981.

———. *Recovering Religious Concepts: Closing Epistemic Divides*. New York: St. Martin's Press, 2000.

Placher, William C. *The Domestication of Transcendence: How Modern Thinking about God Went Wrong*. Louisville, KY: Westminster John Knox Press, 1996.

———. *Narratives of a Vulnerable God: Christ, Theology, and Scripture*. Louisville, KY: Westminster John Knox Press, 1994.

Polkinghorne, Donald E. *Narrative Knowing and the Human Sciences*. Albany, NY: State University of New York Press, 1988.

Pritchard, James B., ed. *Ancient Near Eastern Texts Relating to the Old Testament*. 3rd ed. Princeton, NJ: Princeton University Press, 1969.

Quine, W. V. O., and J. S. Ullian. *The Web of Belief*. New York: McGraw-Hill, 1970.

Rad, Gerhard von. *Old Testament Theology*. Vol. 1. New York: Harper, 1962.

———. *Old Testament Theology*. Vol. 2. New York: Harper, 1965.

———. *Wisdom in Israel*. London: SCM Press, 1972.

Ricoeur, Paul. *Essays on Biblical Interpretation*. Philadelphia: Fortress Press, 1980.

———. *Figuring the Sacred: Religion, Narrative, and Imagination*. Minneapolis: Fortress Press, 1995.

———. *Interpretation Theory: Discourse and the Surplus of Meaning*. Fort Worth: Texas Christian University Press, 1976.

———. *The Rule of Metaphor: Multidisciplinary Studies of the Creation of Meaning in Language*. Toronto: University of Toronto Press, 1979.

———. *The Symbolism of Evil*. Translated by Emerson Buchanan. New York: Harper and Row, 1967.

———. *Time and Narrative*. Vol. 1. Chicago: University of Chicago Press, 1984.

———. *Time and Narrative*. Vol. 2. Chicago: University of Chicago Press, 1985.

———. *Time and Narrative*. Vol. 3. Chicago: University of Chicago Press, 1988.

Sanders, James A. *From Sacred Story to Sacred Text: Canon as Paradigm*. Philadelphia: Fortress Press, 1987.

Scalise, Charles J. *Hermeneutics as Theological Prolegomena: A Canonical Approach*. Macon, GA: Mercer University Press, 1994.

Smith, James K. *Speech and Theology: Language and the Logic of Incarnation*. London: Routledge, 2002.

Steck, Odil Hannes. "Theological Streams of Tradition." In *Tradition and Theology in the Old Testament*, edited by Douglas A. Knight, 183-214. Philadelphia: Fortress Press, 1977.

Stout, Jeffrey. *Ethics after Babel: The Languages of Morals and Their Discontents*. Boston: Beacon Press, 1988.

Stout, Jeffery, and Robert MacSwain. *Grammar and Grace: Reformulations of Aquinas and Wittgenstein*. London: SCM Press, 2004.

Stroup, George W. *The Promise of Narrative Theology: Recovering the Gospel in the Church*. Eugene, OR: Wipf and Stock, 1997.

Tanner, Kathryn. *Economy of Grace*. Minneapolis: Augsburg Fortress Press, 2005.

———. *The Politics of God: Christian Theologies and Social Justice*. Minneapolis: Augsburg Fortress Press, 1992.

———. *Theories of Culture: A New Agenda for Theology*. Minneapolis: Augsburg Fortress Press, 1997.

Taylor, Charles. *Modern Social Imaginaries*. Durham, NC: Duke University Press, 2004.

———. *Sources of the Self: The Making of the Modern Identity*. Cambridge, MA: Harvard University Press, 1989.

Thiemann, Ronald F. *Revelation and Theology: The Gospel as Narrated Promise*. Notre Dame, IN: University of Notre Dame Press, 1985.

Thiselton, Anthony C. *Hermeneutics: An Introduction*. Grand Rapids: Eerdmans, 2009.

———. *The Two Horizons*. Grand Rapids: Eerdmans, 1980.

Toulmin, Stephen. *Cosmopolis: The Hidden Agenda of Modernity*. Chicago: University of Chicago Press, 1990.

Ward, Graham. *Cities of God*. London: Routledge, 2000.

———. *Cultural Transformation and Religious Practice*. Cambridge, UK: Cambridge University Press, 2005.

———. *How the Light Gets In: Ethical Life I*. Oxford, UK: Oxford University Press, 2016.

———. *The Politics of Discipleship*. Grand Rapids: Baker Academic, 2009.

Westphal, Merold. *Whose Community? Which Interpretation? Philosophical Hermeneutics for the Church*. Grand Rapids: Baker Academic, 2009.

Winch, Peter. *Ethics and Action*. London: Routledge and Kegan Paul, 1972.

———. *The Idea of a Social Science and Its Relation to Philosophy*. 1958. Abingdon, UK: Routledge, 2008.

Wittgenstein, Ludwig. *Culture and Value*. Oxford: Basil Blackwell, 1980.

———. *On Certainty*. New York: Basil Blackwell, 1969.

———. *Philosophical Investigations*. Oxford, UK: Basil Blackwell, 1953.

Wright, Nicholas Thomas. *How God Became King: The Forgotten Story of the Gospels*. New York: HarperCollins, 2012.

———. *Jesus and the Victory of God*. Minneapolis: Fortress Press, 1996.

———. *The New Testament and the People of God*. Minneapolis: Fortress Press, 1992.

———. *The Resurrection of the Son of God*. Minneapolis: Fortress Press, 2003.

Yoder, John Howard. *The Politics of Jesus*. Grand Rapids: Eerdmans, 1972.

Zimmerli, Walther. *Old Testament Theology in Outline*. Louisville, KY: John Knox Press, 1978.

———. "Prophetic Proclamation and Reinterpretation." In *Tradition and Theology in the Old Testament*, edited by Douglas A. Knight, 69-100. Philadelphia: Fortress Press, 1977.

www.ingramcontent.com/pod-product-compliance
Lightning Source LLC
Chambersburg PA
CBHW070038100426
42740CB00013B/2727